# The Ultimate Air Fryer Cookbook For Beginners UK

*1500 Days Of Delicious And Affordable Air Fryer Recipes With European Measurement Units And Temperatures*

Alfreda F. Turner

# Copyright © 2023 by Alfreda F. Turner - All rights reserved.

The content contained within this book may not be reproduced, duplicated, or transmitted without direct written permission from the author or the publisher. Under no circumstances will any blame or legal responsibility be held against the publisher, or author, for any damages, reparation, or monetary loss due to the information contained within this book, either directly or indirectly.

**Legal Notice**: This book is copyright protected. It is only for personal use. You cannot amend, distribute, sell, use, quote or paraphrase any part, or the content within this book, without the consent of the author or publisher.

**Disclaimer Notice**: Please note the information contained within this document is for educational and entertainment purposes only. All effort has been executed to present accurate, up to date, reliable, complete information. No warranties of any kind are declared or implied. Readers acknowledge that the author is not engaged in the rendering of legal, financial, medical, or professional advice. The content within this book has been derived from various sources. Please consult a licensed professional before attempting any techniques outlined in this book. By reading this document, the reader agrees that under no circumstances is the author responsible for any losses, direct or indirect, that are incurred as a result of the use of the information contained within this document, including, but not limited to, errors, omissions, or inaccuracies.

# CONTENTS

**Introduction** .................................................................................................. 10

**Chapter 1 Cooking with an Air Fryer** ........................................................ 10

    Why Air Frying? .......................................................................................... 11

    Choosing an Air Fryer ................................................................................. 11

    The Functions of an Air Fryer .................................................................... 11

**Chapter 2 Breakfast & Snacks And Fries Recipes** .................................. 12

    Meaty Egg Cups ......................................................................................... 12

    Loaded Hash Browns ................................................................................. 12

    Potato & Chorizo Frittata ............................................................................ 13

    Easy Air Fryer Sausage .............................................................................. 13

    Healthy Stuffed Peppers ............................................................................. 14

    Cheesy Sausage Breakfast Pockets .......................................................... 14

    Easy Cheesy Scrambled Eggs ................................................................... 15

    Easy Cheese & Bacon Toasties ................................................................. 15

    Mexican Breakfast Burritos ........................................................................ 16

    European Pancakes ................................................................................... 16

    Raspberry Breakfast Pockets .................................................................... 17

    Tangy Breakfast Hash ................................................................................ 17

    French Toast .............................................................................................. 18

    Blanket Breakfast Eggs .............................................................................. 18

    Breakfast Sausage Burgers ....................................................................... 19

    Oozing Baked Eggs ................................................................................... 19

    Egg & Bacon Breakfast Cups .................................................................... 20

    Crunchy Mexican Breakfast Wrap ............................................................. 20

    Blueberry & Lemon Breakfast Muffins ....................................................... 21

    Monte Cristo Breakfast Sandwich ............................................................. 21

# Chapter 3 Sauces & Snack And Appetiser Recipes ............ 22

    Plantain Fries ............................................................................................................ 22

    Baba Ganoush .......................................................................................................... 22

    Air Fryer Hot Dogs .................................................................................................. 23

    Cheesy Taco Crescents ............................................................................................ 23

    Sweet Potato Fries ................................................................................................... 24

    Bacon Smokies ........................................................................................................ 24

    Air Fryer 2-inigrdient Sweet Potato Roll: No Yeast ............................................... 25

    Pao De Queijo ......................................................................................................... 25

    Beetroot Crisps ........................................................................................................ 26

    Pork Jerky ................................................................................................................ 26

    Focaccia Bread ........................................................................................................ 27

    Air Fryer Bacon Wrapped Zucchini Fries ............................................................... 27

    Spring Rolls ............................................................................................................. 28

    Pretzel Bites ............................................................................................................. 28

    Air Fryer Party Snack Mix-"nuts & Bolts" .............................................................. 29

    Stuffed Mushrooms ................................................................................................. 29

    Snack Style Falafel .................................................................................................. 30

    Air Fryer Frozen Breadsticks ................................................................................... 30

    Air Fryer Chili Cheese Hotdogs .............................................................................. 31

    Whole Mini Peppers ................................................................................................ 31

# Chapter 4 Poultry Recipes .................................................................................. 32

    Air Fryer Rosemary Chicken Breast ............................................................................... 32

    Air Fryer Trader Joe's Frozen Kung Pao Chicken ........................................................... 32

    Hawaiian Chicken .............................................................................................................. 33

    Spicy Chicken Wing Drummettes ..................................................................................... 33

    Chicken Milanese .............................................................................................................. 34

    Satay Chicken Skewers ..................................................................................................... 34

    Sticky Chicken Tikka Drumsticks .................................................................................... 35

    Air Fryer Chicken Wings .................................................................................................. 35

    Quick Chicken Nuggets .................................................................................................... 36

    Olive Stained Turkey Breast ............................................................................................. 36

    Cheddar & Bbq Stuffed Chicken ....................................................................................... 37

    Air Fryer Chicken Breast .................................................................................................. 37

    Bbq Chicken Tenders ........................................................................................................ 38

    Air Fryer Frozen Chicken Cordon Bleu ........................................................................... 38

    Buffalo Wings ................................................................................................................... 39

    Air Fryer Rotisserie Chicken ............................................................................................ 39

    Air Fryer Chicken Parmesan ............................................................................................. 40

    Air Fryer Tikka Chicken Breast ........................................................................................ 41

    Air Fryer Chicken Wings With Honey And Sesame ....................................................... 41

    Air Fryer Chicken Tenders ............................................................................................... 42

# Chapter 5 Beef & Lamb And Pork Recipes .......................................... 43

    Steak Popcorn Bites .......................................................................................................... 43

    Chinese Pork With Pineapple ........................................................................................... 43

    Simple Steaks .................................................................................................................... 44

    Air Fryer Rack Of Lamb ................................................................................................... 44

    Beef Stirfry ........................................................................................................................ 45

    Air Fryer Lamb Steaks ...................................................................................................... 45

Italian Meatballs ......................................................................................................... 46

Sticky Asian Beef ........................................................................................................ 46

Pork Chops With Sprouts ............................................................................................ 47

Apricot Lamb Burgers ................................................................................................. 47

Pork With Chinese 5 Spice .......................................................................................... 48

Mini Moroccan Lamb Burgers .................................................................................... 48

Mongolian Beef ........................................................................................................... 49

Salt And Pepper Belly Pork ......................................................................................... 49

Traditional Empanadas ................................................................................................ 50

Air Fryer Bacon-wrapped Asparagus .......................................................................... 50

Pulled Pork, Bacon, And Cheese Sliders .................................................................... 51

Honey & Mustard Meatballs ....................................................................................... 51

Lamb Koftas ................................................................................................................ 52

Beef Nacho Pinwheels ................................................................................................. 52

# Chapter 6 Fish & Seafood Recipes ................................................................. 53

Air Fryer Spicy Bay Scallops ...................................................................................... 53

Lemon Pepper Shrimp ................................................................................................. 53

Air Fryer Orange Shrimp & Broccol ........................................................................... 54

Pesto Salmon ............................................................................................................... 54

Shrimp With Yum Yum Sauce .................................................................................... 55

Fish In Foil .................................................................................................................. 55

Coconut Shrimp .......................................................................................................... 56

Copycat Fish Fingers .................................................................................................. 56

Air Fryer Crab Cakes .................................................................................................. 57

Peppery Lemon Shrimp ............................................................................................... 58

Cod In Parma Ham ...................................................................................................... 58

Garlic Butter Salmon ................................................................................................... 59

Air Fryer Lemon Pepper Shrimp ................................................................................. 59

Fish Sticks With Tartar Sauce Batter ............................................................................................. 60

Air Fryer Fish Fillets ........................................................................................................................ 60

Air Fryer Tuna ................................................................................................................................. 61

Oat & Parmesan Crusted Fish Fillets ............................................................................................. 61

Salmon Patties ................................................................................................................................ 62

Store-cupboard Fishcakes .............................................................................................................. 62

Gluten Free Honey And Garlic Shrimp .......................................................................................... 63

# Chapter 7 Vegetarian & Vegan Recipes ................................................. 63

Lentil Burgers ................................................................................................................................. 63

Paneer Tikka .................................................................................................................................... 64

Rainbow Vegetables ........................................................................................................................ 64

Orange Zingy Cauliflower .............................................................................................................. 65

Spinach And Feta Croissants .......................................................................................................... 65

Air Feyer Breaded Asparagus Fries ................................................................................................ 66

Baked Feta, Tomato & Garlic Pasta ................................................................................................ 66

Air Fryer Parsnips ........................................................................................................................... 67

Vegan Meatballs ............................................................................................................................. 67

Veggie Lasagne ............................................................................................................................... 68

Roast Cauliflower & Broccoli ........................................................................................................ 68

Crispy Potato Peels ......................................................................................................................... 69

Air Fryer Green Beans .................................................................................................................... 69

Roasted Vegetable Pasta ................................................................................................................. 70

Crispy Broccoli ............................................................................................................................... 70

Spring Ratatouille ........................................................................................................................... 71

Roast Vegetables ............................................................................................................................. 71

Air Fryer Muchrooms ..................................................................................................................... 72

Baked Aubergine Slices With Yogurt Dressing ............................................................................. 72

Patatas Bravas ................................................................................................................................. 73

# Chapter 8 Side Dishes Recipes .................................................................. 73

- Spicy Green Beans ..................................................................................... 73
- Air Fryer Eggy Bread .................................................................................. 74
- Cheesy Garlic Asparagus ............................................................................ 74
- Courgette Chips ......................................................................................... 75
- Homemade Croquettes .............................................................................. 75
- Grilled Bacon And Cheese .......................................................................... 76
- Sweet Potato Tots ...................................................................................... 76
- Potato Hay ................................................................................................ 77
- Crispy Cinnamon French Toast .................................................................... 77
- Carrot & Parmesan Chips ........................................................................... 78
- Pumpkin Fries ............................................................................................ 78
- Bbq Beetroot Crisps ................................................................................... 79
- Shishito Peppers ........................................................................................ 79
- Cauliflower With Hot Sauce And Blue Cheese Sauce .................................... 80
- Garlic And Parsley Potatoes ....................................................................... 80
- Cheesy Broccoli ......................................................................................... 81
- Sweet And Sticky Parsnips And Carrots ...................................................... 81
- Zingy Brussels Sprouts ............................................................................... 82
- Ranch-style Potatoes ................................................................................. 82
- Stuffing Filled Pumpkin .............................................................................. 83

# Chapter 9 Desserts Recipes .................................................................. 83

Special Oreos .................................................................................................. 83

Apple Crumble ............................................................................................... 84

Zebra Cake ..................................................................................................... 84

Milk And White Chocolate Chip Air Fryer Donuts With Frosting ................ 85

Fruit Scones ................................................................................................... 86

Strawberry Lemonade Pop Tarts .................................................................... 86

Chocolate Soufflé .......................................................................................... 87

Lava Cakes ..................................................................................................... 87

Thai Fried Bananas ........................................................................................ 88

Key Lime Cupcakes ....................................................................................... 88

Chocolate Dipped Biscuits ............................................................................. 89

Pecan & Molasses Flapjack ........................................................................... 89

Chocolate Souffle .......................................................................................... 90

Banana Maple Flapjack ................................................................................. 90

Tasty Cannoli ................................................................................................. 91

Chocolate Cake .............................................................................................. 92

Lemon Tarts ................................................................................................... 92

Chocolate Orange Muffins ............................................................................. 93

Melting Moments ........................................................................................... 93

Banana Bread ................................................................................................. 94

# Recipe Index .................................................................................... 95

# Introduction

If you have an air fryer, you've already experienced the quick cooking times and ease of use that show why the demand for this revolutionary appliance is so high. If you're still on the fence about buying one, get ready to flex your culinary muscles and get excited about cooking. You'll soon be hooked and using your air fryer to prepare nearly every meal. But what's so special about air frying?

The air fryer can replace your oven, microwave, deep fryer, and dehydrator, and evenly cook delicious meals in a fraction of the time (and electricity costs) you're used to. Air frying makes it easy to feed your family healthy, irresistible meals with just five ingredients or less!

An air fryer can also help you succeed on the keto diet. Typically, fried foods are loaded with carbohydrates, so you might assume you have to avoid them altogether when on a keto diet. But when you use the air fryer, you can get the distinct crunch and mouthwatering taste of your fried favorites without the carbs. And you can choose your own low-carb breading! Another benefit to air frying is how much it shortens cooking time. This is especially crucial when you are hungry, short on time, and running low on supplies—a recipe for cheating on your diet. That's why your air fryer will be your best friend throughout your keto journey and help you stay on track, without venturing outside of a small list of ingredients and pantry staples.

# Chapter 1 Cooking with an Air Fryer

Cooking with an air fryer is as easy as using a microwave. Anybody can do it, and after just a few uses you'll wish you had switched over to this genius method of cooking earlier. This chapter will introduce you to air-frying options and accessories to maximize your cooking time and get delicious, crispy results. It will also explain how to keep your air fryer clean and offer essentials you'll want to stock up on so that you can whip up a delicious meal with just five ingredients or less any day of the week.

While this chapter will cover the basics of air frying, the first step is reading the manual that came with your air fryer. The recent rise in popularity of the appliance means that you'll find a variety of models with different settings and sizes on the market. A thorough knowledge of how to use your specific air fryer is the key to success and will familiarize you with troubleshooting issues as well as safety functions. Read over the manual and wash all parts with warm, soapy water before first use to help you feel ready to unleash your culinary finesse.

# Why Air Frying?

Air frying is increasingly popular because it allows you to quickly and evenly prepare delicious meals with little fat and little effort. Here are just a few of the reasons you'll want to switch to air frying:

• It replaces other cooking appliances. You can use your air fryer in place of your oven, microwave, deep fryer, and dehydrator! Using one small device, you can quickly cook up perfect dishes for every meal without sacrificing flavor.

• It cooks faster than traditional cooking methods. Air frying works by circulating hot air around the cooking chamber. This results in fast and even cooking, using a fraction of the energy of your oven. Most air fryers can be set to a maximum temperature of 400°F, so just about anything you can make in an oven, you can make in an air fryer.

• It uses little to no cooking oil. A main selling point of air fryers is that you can achieve beautifully cooked foods using little to no cooking oil. Even people following the keto diet can appreciate the lower fat content; calorie counts are important if you're following keto for weight loss, or if you track your macros and choose to use your calories otherwise.

• Cleanup is fast. Any method of cooking will dirty your cooker, but your air fryer's smaller cooking chamber and removable basket make thorough cleanup a breeze!

## Choosing an Air Fryer

When choosing an air fryer, the two most important factors to focus on are size and temperature range. Air fryers are usually measured by quart size and range from about 1.2 quarts to 10 or more quarts. Thanks to the number of models available, you can now even find air fryer "ovens"—larger convection oven–type appliances that you can use to cook multiple racks of food at the same time. This book is based on a four-person air fryer with a 3-quart capacity and 1425 watts of power. If you're looking to cook meals to feed a family, you might be interested in at least a 5.3-quart fryer that can be used to beautifully roast an entire chicken. If your counter space is limited, and you're cooking for only one or two, you can make do with a much smaller air fryer. As for temperature range, some air fryers allow you the ability to dehydrate foods because you can cook them at a very low temperature, say 120°F, for a long period of time. Depending on the functions you need, you'll want to make sure your air fryer has the appropriate cooking capacity and temperature range.

## The Functions of an Air Fryer

Most air fryers are equipped with buttons to help you prepare anything, such as grilling the perfect salmon, roasting an entire chicken, or even baking a chocolate cake.

These buttons are programmed to preset times and temperatures based on your specific air fryer. Because of the wide variety of air fryers on the market, all the recipes in this book were created using manual times and temperatures, without preheating. Every air fryer allows you to set these yourself. Still, it is important to know how the cooking programs work on your air fryer and when to use them.

# Chapter 2 Breakfast & Snacks And Fries Recipes

## Meaty Egg Cups

Servings: 4

**Ingredients:**
- 8 slices of toasted sandwich bread
- 2 slices of ham
- 4 eggs
- Salt and pepper to taste
- Butter for greasing

**Directions:**
1. Take 4 ramekins and grease the insides with a little butter
2. Flatten the slices of toast with a rolling pin and arrange inside the ramekins - two in each
3. Line the inside of each ramekin with a slice of ham
4. Crack one egg into each ramekin
5. Season with a little salt and pepper
6. Place the ramekins into the air fryer and cook at 160ºC for 15 minutes
7. Remove from the fryer and wait to cool just slightly
8. Remove and serve

## Loaded Hash Browns

Servings: 4

**Ingredients:**
- 4 large potatoes
- 2 tbsp bicarbonate of soda
- 1 tbsp salt
- 1 tbsp black pepper
- 1 tsp cayenne pepper
- 2 tbsp olive oil
- 1 large chopped onion
- 1 chopped red pepper
- 1 chopped green pepper

**Directions:**
1. Grate the potatoes
2. Squeeze out any water contained within the potatoes
3. Take a large bowl of water and add the potatoes
4. Add the bicarbonate of soda, combine everything and leave to soak for 25 minutes
5. Drain the water away and carefully pat the potatoes to dry
6. Transfer your potatoes into another bowl
7. Add the spices and oil
8. Combining everything well, tossing to coat evenly
9. Place your potatoes into your fryer basket
10. Set to 200ºC and cook for 10 minutes
11. Give the potatoes a shake and add the peppers and the onions
12. Cook for another 10 minutes

# Potato & Chorizo Frittata

Servings: 2

**Ingredients:**
- 3 eggs
- 1 sliced chorizo sausage
- 1 potato, boiled and cubed
- 50g feta cheese
- 50g frozen sweetcorn
- A pinch of salt
- 1 tbsp olive oil

**Directions:**
1. Add a little olive oil to the frying basket
2. Add the corn, potato, and sliced chorizo to the basket
3. Cook at 180°C until the sausage is a little brown
4. In a small bowl, beat together the eggs with a little seasoning
5. Pour the eggs into the pan
6. Crumble the feta on top
7. Cook for 5 minutes
8. Remove and serve in slices

# Easy Air Fryer Sausage

Servings: 5

**Ingredients:**
- 5 uncooked sausages
- 1 tbsp mustard
- Salt and pepper for seasoning

**Directions:**
1. Line the basket of your fryer with parchment paper
2. Arrange the sausages inside the basket
3. Set to 180°C and cook for 15 minutes
4. Turn the sausages over and cook for another 5 minutes
5. Remove and cool
6. Drizzle the mustard over the top and season to your liking

# Healthy Stuffed Peppers

Servings: 2

**Ingredients:**
- 1 large bell pepper, deseeded and cut into halves
- 1 tsp olive oil
- 4 large eggs
- Salt and pepper to taste

**Directions:**
1. Take your peppers and rub a little olive oil on the edges
2. Into each pepper, crack one egg and season with salt and pepper
3. You will need to insert a trivet into your air fryer to hold the peppers, and then arrange the peppers evenly
4. Set your fryer to 200°C and cook for 13 minutes
5. Once cooked, remove and serve with a little more seasoning, if required

# Cheesy Sausage Breakfast Pockets

Servings: 2

**Ingredients:**
- 1 packet of regular puff pastry
- 4 sausages, cooked and crumbled into pieces
- 5 eggs
- 50g cooked bacon
- 50g grated cheddar cheese

**Directions:**
1. Scramble your eggs in your usual way
2. Add the sausage and the bacon as you are cooking the eggs and combine well
3. Take your pastry sheets and cut rectangular shapes
4. Add a little of the egg and meat mixture to one half of each pastry piece
5. Fold the rectangles over and use a fork to seal down the edges
6. Place your pockets into your air fryer and cook at 190°C for 10 minutes
7. Allow to cool before serving

# Easy Cheesy Scrambled Eggs

Servings: 1

**Ingredients:**
- 1 tbsp butter
- 2 eggs
- 100g grated cheese
- 2 tbsp milk
- Salt and pepper for seasoning

**Directions:**
1. Add the butter inside the air fryer pan and cook at 220°C until the butter has melted
2. Add the eggs and milk to a bowl and combine, seasoning to your liking
3. Pour the eggs into the butter panned cook for 3 minutes, stirring around lightly to scramble
4. Add the cheese and cook for another 2 more minutes

# Easy Cheese & Bacon Toasties

Servings: 2

**Ingredients:**
- 4 slices of sandwich bread
- 2 slices of cheddar cheese
- 5 slices of pre-cooked bacon
- 1 tbsp melted butter
- 2 slices of mozzarella cheese

**Directions:**
1. Take the bread and spread the butter onto one side of each slice
2. Place one slice of bread into the fryer basket, buttered side facing downwards
3. Place the cheddar on top, followed by the bacon, mozzarella and the other slice of bread on top, buttered side upwards
4. Set your fryer to 170°C
5. Cook for 4 minutes and then turn over and cook for another 3 minutes
6. Serve whilst still hot

# **Mexican Breakfast Burritos**

Servings: 6

**Ingredients:**
- 6 scrambled eggs
- 6 medium tortillas
- Half a minced red pepper
- 8 sausages, cut into cubes and browned
- 4 pieces of bacon, pre-cooked and cut into pieces
- 65g grated cheese of your choice
- A small amount of olive oil for cooking

**Directions:**
1. Into a regular mixing bowl, combine the eggs, bell pepper, bacon pieces, the cheese, and the browned sausage, giving everything a good stir
2. Take your first tortilla and place half a cup of the mixture into the middle, folding up the top and bottom and rolling closed
3. Repeat until all your tortillas have been used
4. Arrange the burritos into the bottom of your fryer and spray with a little oil
5. Cook the burritos at 170°C for 5 minutes

# **European Pancakes**

Servings: 5

**Ingredients:**
- 3 large eggs
- 130g flour
- 140ml whole milk
- 2 tbsp unsweetened apple sauce
- A pinch of salt

**Directions:**
1. Set your fryer to 200°C and add five ramekins inside to heat up
2. Place all your ingredients inside a blender to combine
3. Spray the ramekins with a little cooking spray
4. Pour the batter into the ramekins carefully
5. Fry for between 6-8 minutes, depending on your preference
6. Serve with your favourite toppings

# Raspberry Breakfast Pockets

Servings: 1

**Ingredients:**

- 2 slices of sandwich bread
- 1 tbsp soft cream cheese
- 1 tbsp raspberry jam
- 1 tbsp milk
- 1 egg

**Directions:**

1. Take one slice of the bread and add one tablespoon of jam into the middle
2. Take the second slice and add the cream cheese into the middle
3. Using a blunt knife, spread the jam and the cheese across the bread, but don't go to the outer edges
4. Take a small bowl and whisk the eggs and the milk together
5. Set your fryer to 190°C and spray with a little oil
6. Dip your sandwich into the egg and arrange inside your fryer
7. Cook for 5 minutes on the first side, turn and cook for another 2 minutes

# Tangy Breakfast Hash

Servings: 6

**Ingredients:**

- 2 tbsp olive oil
- 2 sweet potatoes, cut into cubes
- 1 tbsp smoked paprika
- 1 tsp salt
- 1 tsp black pepper
- 2 slices of bacon, cut into small pieces

**Directions:**

1. Preheat your air fryer to 200°C
2. Pour the olive oil into a large mixing bowl
3. Add the bacon, seasonings, potatoes and toss to evenly coat
4. Transfer the mixture into the air fryer and cook for 12-16 minutes
5. Stir after 10 minutes and continue to stir periodically for another 5 minutes

# French Toast

Servings: 2

**Ingredients:**
- 2 beaten eggs
- 2 tbsp softened butter
- 4 slices of sandwich bread
- 1 tsp cinnamon
- 1 tsp nutmeg
- 1 tsp ground cloves
- 1 tsp maple syrup

**Directions:**
1. Preheat your fryer to 180°C
2. Take a bowl and add the eggs, salt, cinnamon, nutmeg, and cloves, combining well
3. Take your bread and butter each side, cutting into strips
4. Dip the bread slices into the egg mixture
5. Arrange each slice into the basket of your fryer
6. Cook for 2 minutes
7. Take the basket out and spray with a little cooking spray
8. Turn over the slices and place back into the fryer
9. Cook for 4 minutes
10. Remove and serve with maple syrup

# Blanket Breakfast Eggs

Servings: 2

**Ingredients:**
- 2 eggs
- 2 slices of sandwich bread
- Olive oil spray
- Salt and pepper to taste

**Directions:**
1. Preheat your air fryer to 190°C and spray with a little oil
2. Meanwhile, take your bread and cut a hole into the middle of each piece
3. Place one slice inside your fryer and crack one egg into the middle
4. Season with a little salt and pepper
5. Cook for 5 minutes, before turning over and cooking for a further 2 minutes
6. Remove the first slice and repeat the process with the remaining slice of bread and egg

# Breakfast Sausage Burgers

Servings: 2

**Ingredients:**
- 8 links of your favourite sausage
- Salt and pepper to taste

**Directions:**
1. Remove the sausage from the skins and use a fork to create a smooth mixture
2. Season to your liking
3. Shape the sausage mixture into burgers or patties
4. Preheat your air fryer to 260°C
5. Arrange the burgers in the fryer, so they are not touching each other
6. Cook for 8 minutes
7. Serve still warm

# Oozing Baked Eggs

Servings: 2

**Ingredients:**
- 4 eggs
- 140g smoked gouda cheese, cut into small pieces
- Salt and pepper to taste

**Directions:**
1. You will need two ramekin dishes and spray each one before using
2. Crack two eggs into each ramekin dish
3. Add half of the Gouda cheese to each dish
4. Season and place into the air fryer
5. Cook at 350°C for 15 minutes, until the eggs are cooked as you like them

## Egg & Bacon Breakfast Cups

Servings: 8

**Ingredients:**
- 6 eggs
- 1 chopped red pepper
- 1 chopped green pepper
- 1 chopped yellow pepper
- 2 tbsp double cream
- 50g chopped spinach
- 50g grated cheddar cheese
- 50g grated mozzarella cheese
- 3 slices of cooked bacon, crumbled into pieces

**Directions:**
1. Take a large mixing bowl and crack the eggs
2. Add the cream and season with a little salt and pepper, combining everything well
3. Add the peppers, spinach, onions, both cheeses, and the crumbled bacon, combining everything once more
4. You will need silicone moulds or cups for this part, and you should pour equal amounts of the mixture into 8 cups
5. Cook at 150°C for around 12 or 15 minutes, until the eggs are cooked properly

## Crunchy Mexican Breakfast Wrap

Servings: 2

**Ingredients:**
- 2 large tortillas
- 2 corn tortillas
- 1 sliced jalapeño pepper
- 4 tbsp ranchero sauce
- 1 sliced avocado
- 25g cooked pinto beans

**Directions:**
1. Take each of your large tortillas and add the egg, jalapeño, sauce, the corn tortillas, the avocado and the pinto beans, in that order. If you want to add more sauce at this point, you can
2. Fold over your wrap to make sure that nothing escapes
3. Place each wrap into your fryer and cook at 190°C for 6 minutes
4. Remove your wraps and place in the oven, cooking for a further 5 minutes at 180°C, until crispy
5. Place each wrap into a frying pan and crisp a little more on a low heat, for a couple of minutes on each side

# **Blueberry & Lemon Breakfast Muffins**

Servings: 12

**Ingredients:**
- 315g self raising flour
- 65g sugar
- 120ml double cream
- 2 tbsp of light cooking oil
- 2 eggs
- 125g blueberries
- The zest and juice of a lemon
- 1 tsp vanilla

**Directions:**
1. Take a small bowl and mix the self raising flour and sugar together
2. Take another bowl and mix together the oil, juice, eggs, cream, and vanilla
3. Add this mixture to the flour mixture and blend together
4. Add the blueberries and fold
5. You will need individual muffin holders, silicone works best. Spoon the mixture into the holders
6. Cook at 150°C for 10 minutes
7. Check at the halfway point to check they're not cooking too fast
8. Remove and allow to cool

# **Monte Cristo Breakfast Sandwich**

Servings: 4

**Ingredients:**
- 1 egg
- 2 slices of sandwich bread
- 1/4 tsp vanilla extract
- 4 slices of sliced Swiss cheese
- 4 slices of sliced deli ham
- 4 slices of sliced turkey
- 1 tsp melted butter
- Powdered sugar for serving

**Directions:**
1. In a small bowl, mix together the egg and vanilla extract, combining well
2. Take your bread and assemble your sandwich, starting with a slice of cheese, then the ham, turkey, and then another slice of the cheese, with the other slice of bread on the top
3. Compress the sandwich a little, so it cooks better
4. Take a piece of cooking foil and brush over it with the butter
5. Take your sandwich and dip each side into the egg mixture, leaving it to one side for around half a minute
6. Place the sandwich on the foil and place it inside your fryer
7. Cook at 200°C for around 10 minutes, before turning the sandwich over and cooking for another 8 minutes
8. Transfer your sandwich onto a plate and sprinkle with a little powdered sugar

# Chapter 3 Sauces & Snack And Appetiser Recipes

## Plantain Fries

Servings: 2
Cooking Time: X
**Ingredients:**
- 1 ripe plantain (yellow and brown outside skin)
- 1 teaspoon olive oil
- ¼ teaspoon salt

**Directions:**
1. Preheat the air-fryer to 180°C/350°F.
2. Peel the plantain and slice into fries about 6 x 1 cm/2½ x ½ in. Toss the fries in oil and salt, making sure every fry is coated.
3. Tip into the preheated air-fryer in a single layer (you may need to cook them in two batches, depending on the size of your air-fryer) and air-fry for 13–14 minutes until brown on the outside and soft on the inside. Serve immediately.

## Baba Ganoush

Servings: 4
Cooking Time: X
**Ingredients:**
- 1 large aubergine/eggplant, sliced in half lengthways
- ½ teaspoon salt
- 5 tablespoons olive oil
- 1 bulb garlic
- 30 g/2 tablespoons tahini or nut butter
- 2 tablespoons freshly squeezed lemon juice
- ½ teaspoon ground cumin
- ¼ teaspoon smoked paprika
- salt and freshly ground black pepper
- 3 tablespoons freshly chopped flat-leaf parsley

**Directions:**
1. Preheat the air-fryer to 200°C/400°F.
2. Lay the aubergine/eggplant halves cut side up. Sprinkle over the salt, then drizzle over 1 tablespoon of oil. Cut the top off the garlic bulb, brush the exposed cloves with a little olive oil, then wrap in foil. Place the aubergine/eggplant and foil-wrapped garlic in the preheated air-fryer and air-fry for 15–20 minutes until the inside of the aubergine is soft and buttery in texture.
3. Scoop the flesh of the aubergine into a bowl. Squeeze out about 1 tablespoon of the cooked garlic and add to the bowl with the remaining 4 tablespoons of olive oil, the tahini/nut butter, lemon juice, spices and salt and pepper to taste. Mix well and serve with fresh flat-leaf parsley sprinkled over.

# Air Fryer Hot Dogs

Servings: 6
Cooking Time: 5 Mints
**Ingredients:**
- 6 hot dogs
- 6 hot dog buns

**Directions:**
1. Place hot dogs in basket of air fryer. Cook at 200°C/400°F for 4 minutes. Remove from basket.
2. Place buns in basket and cook at 200°C/400°F.
3. Place hot dogs in buns and top with desired toppings

# Cheesy Taco Crescents

Servings: 8
**Ingredients:**
- 1 can Pillsbury crescent sheets, or alternative
- 4 Monterey Jack cheese sticks
- 150g browned minced beef
- ½ pack taco seasoning mix

**Directions:**
1. Preheat the air fryer to 200°C
2. Combine the minced beef and the taco seasoning, warm in the microwave for about 2 minutes
3. Cut the crescent sheets into 8 equal squares
4. Cut the cheese sticks in half
5. Add half a cheese stick to each square, and 2 tablespoons of mince
6. Roll up the dough and pinch at the ends to seal
7. Place in the air fryer and cook for 5 minutes
8. Turnover and cook for another 3 minutes

# Sweet Potato Fries

Servings: 4
Cooking Time: X

**Ingredients:**
- 2 medium sweet potatoes
- 2 teaspoons olive oil
- ½ teaspoon salt
- ½ teaspoon chilli/hot red pepper flakes
- ½ teaspoon smoked paprika

**Directions:**
1. Preheat the air-fryer to 190°C/375°F.
2. Peel the sweet potatoes and slice into fries about 1 x 1 cm/½ x ½ in. by the length of the potato. Toss the sweet potato fries in the oil, salt, chilli and paprika, making sure every fry is coated.
3. Tip into the preheated air-fryer in a single layer (you may need to cook them in two batches, depending on the size of your air-fryer). Air-fry for 10 minutes, turning once halfway during cooking. Serve immediately.

# Bacon Smokies

Servings: 8

**Ingredients:**
- 150g little smokies (pieces)
- 150g bacon
- 50g brown sugar
- Toothpicks

**Directions:**
1. Cut the bacon strips into thirds
2. Put the brown sugar into a bowl
3. Coat the bacon with the sugar
4. Wrap the bacon around the little smokies and secure with a toothpick
5. Heat the air fryer to 170°C
6. Place in the air fryer and cook for 10 minutes until crispy

# Air Fryer 2-inigrdient Sweet Potato Roll: No Yeast

Servings: 2-4
Cooking Time: 14 Mints
**Ingredients:**
- 1 cup (240 ml) cooked sweet potato , mashed
- 1 cup (240 ml) self rising flour
- oil spray , for basket & rolls

**Directions:**
1. In bowl, combine sweet potato and flour. Stir with a fork until a dough ball forms. Make sure to scrape all the flour and sweet potato along the sides of the bowl.
2. On a lightly floured surface, knead the soft dough ball for about 1 minute, or until smooth. Don't keep adding too much flour to the dough or else it will be tough and hard. You want to keep the dough soft and pliable, so don't over-knead it.
3. Cut the dough into 6 equal pieces. Roll the dough between your hands to form 6 balls. Let the dough balls rest for about 30 minutes (they will also rise slightly).
4. Spray air fryer basket or tray with oil. Gently place dough balls in the basket, evenly spaced apart. Lightly spray the tops of the dough balls with oil.
5. Air Fry at 330°F/165°C for 10-14 minutes or until the rolls are cooked through. Allow them to cool and serve with butter or as small slider or sandwich buns.

# Pao De Queijo

Servings: 20
**Ingredients:**
- 150g sweet starch
- 150g sour starch
- 50ml milk
- 25ml water
- 25ml olive oil
- 1 tsp salt
- 2 eggs
- 100g grated cheese
- 50g grated parmesan

**Directions:**
1. Preheat the air fryer to 170°C
2. Mix the starch together in a bowl until well mixed
3. Add olive oil, milk and water to a pan, bring to the boil and reduce the heat
4. Add the starch and mix until all the liquid is absorbed
5. Add the eggs and mix to a dough
6. Add the cheeses and mix well
7. Form the dough into balls
8. Line the air fryer with parchment paper
9. Bake in the air fryer for 8-10 minutes

# Beetroot Crisps

Servings: 2

**Ingredients:**
- 3 medium beetroots
- 2 tbsp oil
- Salt to taste

**Directions:**
1. Peel and thinly slice the beetroot
2. Coat with the oil and season with salt
3. Preheat the air fryer to 200ºC
4. Place in the air fryer and cook for 12-18 minutes until crispy

# Pork Jerky

Servings: 35

**Ingredients:**
- 300g mince pork
- 1 tbsp oil
- 1 tbsp sriracha
- 1 tbsp soy
- ½ tsp pink curing salt
- 1 tbsp rice vinegar
- ½ tsp salt
- ½ tsp pepper
- ½ tsp onion powder

**Directions:**
1. Mix all ingredients in a bowl until combined
2. Refrigerate for about 8 hours
3. Shape into sticks and place in the air fryer
4. Heat the air fryer to 160ºC
5. Cook for 1 hour turn then cook for another hour
6. Turn again and cook for another hour
7. Cover with paper and sit for 8 hours

# Focaccia Bread

Servings: 8

**Ingredients:**
- 500g pizza dough
- 3 tbsp olive oil
- 2-3 garlic cloves, chopped
- ¼ tsp red pepper flakes
- 50g parsley
- 1 tsp basil
- 100g chopped red peppers
- 60g black olives halved
- 60g green olives halved
- Salt and pepper to taste

**Directions:**
1. Preheat the air fryer to 180°C, make indentations in the pizza dough with your finger tips and set aside
2. Heat the olive oil in a pan add the garlic and cook for a few minutes, add the remaining ingredients and cook for another 5-8 minutes not letting the oil get too hot
3. Spread the oil mix over the dough with a spatula
4. Place in the air fryer and cook for 12-15 minutes


# Air Fryer Bacon Wrapped Zucchini Fries

Servings: 2
Cooking Time: 10 Mints

**Ingredients:**
- 454 g zucchini (2 small-medium zucchini)
- 8 slices bacon, (cut in half lengthwise) (or as much bacon as needed)
- oil spray
- 2 teaspoons garlic powder
- salt, to taste
- black pepper, to taste

**Directions:**
1. Cut the zucchinis in half lengthwise and then into wedges, 1-inch (2.5cm) at the base (usually quartered for small-medium sized zucchini). Lightly spray zucchini with oil. Season all sides with garlic powder, salt and pepper.
2. Wrap with bacon and then season with extra black pepper (optional). Toothpick the bacon into the zucchini to stay in place, and then put in the air fryer basket/tray.
3. Air Fry at 380°F/190°C for 10-16 minutes or until the bacon is crispy to your liking. Flip zucchini half way through cooking. Allow to cool for a couple minutes before serving (zucchini will be very hot). Remove toothpicks before eating

# Spring Rolls

Servings: 20

**Ingredients:**

- 160g dried rice noodles
- 1 tsp sesame oil
- 300g minced beef
- 200g frozen vegetables
- 1 onion, diced
- 3 cloves garlic, crushed
- 1 tsp soy sauce
- 1 tbsp vegetable oil
- 1 pack egg roll wrappers

**Directions:**

1. Soak the noodles in a bowl of water until soft
2. Add the minced beef, onion, garlic and vegetables to a pan and cook for 6 minutes
3. Remove from the heat, stir in the noodles and add the soy
4. Heat the air fryer to 175°C
5. Add a diagonal strip of filling in each egg roll wrapper
6. Fold the top corner over the filling, fold in the two side corners
7. Brush the centre with water and roll to seal
8. Brush with vegetable oil, place in the air fryer and cook for about 8 minutes until browned

# Pretzel Bites

Servings: 2

**Ingredients:**

- 650g flour
- 2.5 tsp active dry yeast
- 260ml hot water
- 1 tsp salt
- 4 tbsp melted butter
- 2 tbsp sugar

**Directions:**

1. Take a large bowl and add the flour, sugar and salt
2. Take another bowl and combine the hot water and yeast, stirring until the yeast has dissolved
3. Then, add the yeast mixture to the flour mixture and use your hands to combine
4. Knead for 2 minutes
5. Cover the bowl with a kitchen towel for around half an hour
6. Divide the dough into 6 pieces
7. Preheat the air fryer to 260°C
8. Take each section of dough and tear off a piece, rolling it in your hands to create a rope shape, that is around 1" in thickness
9. Cut into 2" strips
10. Place the small dough balls into the air fryer and leave a little space in-between
11. Cook for 6 minutes
12. Once cooked, remove and brush with melted butter and sprinkle salt on top

# Air Fryer Party Snack Mix-"nuts & Bolts"

Servings: 4
Cooking Time: 15 Mints

**Ingredients:**
- 480 ml toasted rice, wheat or corn cereal (choose any one or combo)
- 120 ml nuts , your choice – peanuts, cashews, walnuts, etc.
- 120 ml mini pretzels or sticks
- 2 Tablespoons butter , melted
- 1 Tablespoon Worcestershire sauce
- 1/2 teaspoon salt if not using a salted flavoring option, or to taste
- FLAVORING OPTIONS (CHOOSE 1) (IF SEASONING IS SALTY, REDUCE OR ELIMINATE SALT IN RECIPE TO TASTE)
- 2 teaspoons Ranch seasoning mix (for salt lovers, use 15ml)
- 2 teaspoons Everything Bagel seasoning
- 2 teaspoons BBQ seasoning
- 1-2 teaspoons Curry Powder
- 2 teaspoons Steak seasoning

**Directions:**
1. In a large bowl, whisk together the melted butter, Worcestershire sauce, salt and/ or any flavoring options.
2. Add the cereal, nuts and pretzels to the seasoned butter. Stir to completely coat the cereal with the butter mix. Taste for flavor and adjust to your preference.
3. Spread the coated cereal mix out evenly in the air fryer basket/tray.
4. Air Fry at 250°F/120°C for 12-16 minutes, tossing and shaking every 5 minutes. Allow to cool completely and then serve.

# Stuffed Mushrooms

Servings: 24

**Ingredients:**
- 24 mushrooms
- ½ pepper, sliced
- ½ diced onion
- 1 small carrot, diced
- 200g grated cheese
- 2 slices bacon, diced
- 100g sour cream

**Directions:**
1. Place the mushroom stems, pepper, onion, carrot and bacon in a pan and cook for about 5 minutes
2. Stir in cheese and sour cream, cook until well combined
3. Heat the air fryer to 175°C
4. Add stuffing to each of the mushrooms
5. Place in the air fryer and cook for 8 minutes

# Snack Style Falafel

Servings: 15

**Ingredients:**
- 150g dry garbanzo beans
- 300g coriander
- 75g flat leaf parsley
- 1 red onion, quartered
- 1 clove garlic
- 2 tbsp chickpea flour
- Cooking spray
- 1 tbsp cumin
- 1 tbsp coriander
- 1 tbsp sriracha
- ½ tsp baking powder
- Salt and pepper to taste
- ¼ tsp baking soda

**Directions:**
1. Add all ingredients apart from the baking soda and baking powder to a food processor and blend well
2. Cover and rest for 1 hour
3. Heat air fryer to 190°C
4. Add baking powder and baking soda to mix and combine
5. Form mix into 15 equal balls
6. Spray air fryer with cooking spray
7. Add to air fryer and cook for 8-10 minutes

# Air Fryer Frozen Breadsticks

Servings: 4
Cooking Time: 10 Mints

**Ingredients:**
- 4 Frozen Breadsticks

**Directions:**
1. Place the frozen breadsticks in the air fryer basket and spread in an even layer
2. Air Fry at 340°F/170°C for 5 minutes. Flip the breadsticks over. Continue to Air Fry at 340°F/170°C for another 1-5 minutes or until cooked to your desired golden crispness. If you're cooking only 1-2 breadsticks it might take about 5-6 minutes total time, depending on how crisp you like them. Test a piece first and you'll know more of what your preferred timing is like.

# **Air Fryer Chili Cheese Hotdogs**

Servings: 4
Cooking Time: 10 Mints
**Ingredients:**
- 4 hot dog buns
- 4 hot dogs
- 240 ml chili
- 57 g shredded cheddar cheese
- oil for spraying

**Directions:**
1. Add a light spray or brush of oil on the hot dogs. Place the hot dogs in the air fryer basket.
2. Air Fry at 380°F/190°C for 8-10 minutes depending on your preferred texture and size of hot dogs. If you like your hot dogs extra crispy, air fry at 400°F for about 6-8 minutes. Flip the hot dogs half way through cooking.
3. Heat the chili while the hot dogs cook. Set aside.
4. Place hot dogs in buns then add chili and cheese on top. Cook in the air fryer for about one minute to warm and crisp the bread, cheese and chili.

# **Whole Mini Peppers**

Servings: 2
Cooking Time: X
**Ingredients:**
- 9 whole mini (bell) peppers
- 1 teaspoon olive oil
- ¼ teaspoon salt

**Directions:**
1. Preheat the air-fryer to 180°C/350°F.
2. Place the peppers in a baking dish that fits in for your air-fryer and drizzle over the oil, then sprinkle over the salt.
3. Add the dish to the preheated air-fryer and air-fry for 10–12 minutes, depending on how 'chargrilled' you like your peppers.

# Chapter 4 Poultry Recipes

## Air Fryer Rosemary Chicken Breast

Servings: 2
Cooking Time: 20 Mints
**Ingredients:**
- 2 chicken breasts (1 per person)
- Spray oil
- Salt and pepper
- 1/4 teaspoon smoked paprika
- 1/4 teaspoon garlic salt or garlic powder
- 1 spray of rosemary

**Directions:**
1. Remove the rosemary leaves from the sprig and chop finely.
2. Add to a bowl with the salt, pepper, garlic powder and a few sprays of oil, or 1/4 teaspoon. Mix well.
3. Brush this mix onto both sides of your chicken breast.
4. Add to the air fryer basket. Cook at 180°C/360°F for 10 minutes.
5. Turn over and spray lightly with oil again if needed. Cook at 180°C/360°F for another 10 minutes.
6. Check that the internal temperature of the rosemary chicken breast is a minimum of 74°C/165°F and then remove from the air fryer.

## Air Fryer Trader Joe's Frozen Kung Pao Chicken

Servings: 5
Cooking Time: 15 Mints
**Ingredients:**
- 652 g Trader Joe's Frozen Kung Pao Chicken
- optional – chopped cilantro &/or green onion , for garnish
- oil spray, for the veggie

**Directions:**
1. Place the frozen orange chicken in the air fryer basket and spread out into a single even layer. No oil spray is needed. Set the sauce, vegetables, and peanuts aside (do not sauce the chicken yet).
2. Air Fry at 380°F/195°C for 8 minutes. Add the vegetables (if you like the peanuts toastier you can add them now too) and shake/stir to combine with the chicken pieces. Spray with oil spray to lightly coat the vegetables.
3. While the chicken and vegetables air fry: Warm the sauce in microwave or on stovetop until heated through.
4. Continue to Air Fry at 380°F/195°C for another 3-6 minutes or until heated through.
5. Toss cooked chicken with as much sauce as you like, peanuts, optional cilantro and/or green onion and serve.

# Hawaiian Chicken

Servings: 2

**Ingredients:**
- 2 chicken breasts
- 1 tbsp butter
- A pinch of salt and pepper
- 160ml pineapple juice
- 25g brown sugar
- 3 tbsp soy sauce
- 2 tsp water
- 1 clove of garlic, minced
- 1 tsp grated ginger
- 2 tsp cornstarch

**Directions:**
1. Preheat the air fryer to 260°C
2. Take a bowl and combine the butter and salt and pepper
3. Cover the chicken with the butter and cook in the fryer for 15 minutes, turning halfway
4. Remove and allow to rest for 5 minutes
5. Take another bowl and mix together the pineapple juice, soy sauce, garlic, ginger, and brown sugar
6. Transfer to a saucepan and simmer for 5 minutes
7. Combine the water and cornstarch and add to the sauce, stirring continually for another minute
8. Slice the chicken into strips and pour the sauce over the top

# Spicy Chicken Wing Drummettes

Servings: 4

**Ingredients:**
- 10 large chicken drummettes
- Cooking spray
- 100ml rice vinegar
- 3 tbsp honey
- 2 tbsp unsalted chicken stock
- 1 tbsp lower sodium soy sauce
- 1 tbsp toasted sesame oil
- ⅜ tsp crushed red pepper
- 1 garlic clove, finely chopped
- 2 tbsp chopped, unsalted, roasted peanuts
- 1 tbsp chopped fresh chives

**Directions:**
1. Coat the chicken in cooking spray and place inside the air fryer
2. Cook at 200°C for 30 minutes
3. Take a mixing bowl and combine the vinegar, honey, stock, soy sauce, oil, crushed red pepper and garlic
4. Cook to a simmer, until a syrup consistency is achieved
5. Coat the chicken in this mixture and sprinkle with peanuts and chives

# Chicken Milanese

Servings: 4

**Ingredients:**

- 130 g/1¾ cups dried breadcrumbs (gluten-free if you wish, see page 9)
- 50 g/⅔ cup grated Parmesan
- 1 teaspoon dried basil
- ½ teaspoon dried thyme
- ¼ teaspoon freshly ground black pepper
- 1 egg, beaten
- 4 tablespoons plain/all-purpose flour (gluten-free if you wish)
- 4 boneless chicken breasts

**Directions:**

1. Combine the breadcrumbs, cheese, herbs and pepper in a bowl. In a second bowl beat the egg, and in the third bowl have the plain/all-purpose flour. Dip each chicken breast first into the flour, then the egg, then the seasoned breadcrumbs.
2. Preheat the air-fryer to 180ºC/350ºF.
3. Add the breaded chicken breasts to the preheated air-fryer and air-fry for 12 minutes. Check the internal temperature of the chicken has reached at least 74ºC/165ºF using a meat thermometer – if not, cook for another few minutes.

# Satay Chicken Skewers

Servings: 4

**Ingredients:**

- 3 chicken breasts, chopped into 3 x 3-cm/1¼ x 1¼-in. cubes
- MARINADE
- 200 ml/¾ cup canned coconut milk (including the thick part from the can)
- 1 plump garlic clove, finely chopped
- 2 teaspoons freshly grated ginger
- 2 tablespoons soy sauce
- 1 heaped tablespoon peanut butter
- 1 tablespoon maple syrup
- 1 tablespoon mild curry powder
- 1 tablespoon fish sauce

**Directions:**

1. Mix the marinade ingredients thoroughly in a bowl, then toss in the chopped chicken and stir to coat thoroughly. Leave in the fridge to marinate for at least 4 hours.
2. Preheat the air-fryer to 190ºC/375ºF.
3. Thread the chicken onto 8 metal skewers. Add to the preheated air-fryer (you may need to cook these in two batches, depending on the size of your air-fryer). Air-fry for 10 minutes. Check the internal temperature of the chicken has reached at least 74ºC/165ºF using a meat thermometer – if not, cook for another few minutes and then serve.

## **Sticky Chicken Tikka Drumsticks**

Servings: 4

**Ingredients:**

- 12 chicken drumsticks
- MARINADE
- 100 g/½ cup Greek yogurt
- 2 tablespoons tikka paste
- 2 teaspoons ginger preserve
- freshly squeezed juice of ½ a lemon
- ¾ teaspoon salt

**Directions:**

1. Make slices across each of the drumsticks with a sharp knife. Mix the marinade ingredients together in a bowl, then add the drumsticks. Massage the marinade into the drumsticks, then leave to marinate in the fridge overnight or for at least 6 hours.
2. Preheat the air-fryer to 200°C/400°F.
3. Lay the drumsticks on an air-fryer liner or a piece of pierced parchment paper. Place the paper and drumsticks in the preheated air-fryer. Air-fry for 6 minutes, then turn over and cook for a further 6 minutes. Check the internal temperature of the drumsticks has reached at least 75°C/167°F using a meat thermometer – if not, cook for another few minutes and then serve.

## **Air Fryer Chicken Wings**

Servings: 4
Cooking Time: 10 Mints

**Ingredients:**

- 900 g chicken wings
- Salt
- Freshlyground black pepper
- Nonstick cooking spray
- 60 ml hot sauce
- 57 g/4 tbsp. melted butter
- 1 tsp. Worcestershire sauce
- 1/2 tsp. garlic powder
- Blue cheese dressing, for serving

**Directions:**

1. Season wings all over with salt and pepper, and coat the inside of air fryer with nonstick cooking spray.
2. Set air fryer to 190°C/375°F and cook wings 12 minutes. Remove the air fryer tray, flip wings, and cook 12 minutes more. Increase heat to 200°C/400°F and cook 5 minutes more.
3. Meanwhile, in a large bowl, whisk to combine hot sauce, butter, Worcestershire sauce, and garlic powder. Add cooked wings and toss gently to coat. Serve hot with blue cheese dressing for dipping

# Quick Chicken Nuggets

Servings: 4

**Ingredients:**
- 500g chicken tenders
- 25g ranch salad dressing mixture
- 2 tbsp plain flour
- 100g breadcrumbs
- 1 egg, beaten
- Olive oil spray

**Directions:**
1. Take a large mixing bowl and arrange the chicken inside
2. Sprinkle the seasoning over the top and ensure the chicken is evenly coated
3. Place the chicken to one side for around 10 minutes
4. Add the flour into a resealable bag
5. Crack the egg into a small mixing bowl and whisk
6. Pour the breadcrumbs onto a medium sized plate
7. Transfer the chicken into the resealable bag and coat with the flour, giving it a good shake
8. Remove the chicken and dip into the egg, and then rolling it into the breadcrumbs, coating evenly
9. Repeat with all pieces of the chicken
10. Heat your air fryer to 200°C
11. Arrange the chicken inside the fryer and add a little olive oil spray to avoid sticking
12. Cook for 4 minutes, before turning over and cooking for another 4 minutes
13. Remove and serve whilst hot

# Olive Stained Turkey Breast

Servings: 14

**Ingredients:**
- The brine from a can of olives
- 150ml buttermilk
- 300g boneless and skinless turkey breasts
- 1 sprig fresh rosemary
- 2 sprigs fresh thyme

**Directions:**
1. Take a mixing bowl and combine the olive brine and buttermilk
2. Pour the mixture over the turkey breast
3. Add the rosemary and thyme sprigs
4. Place into the refrigerator for 8 hours
5. Remove from the fridge and let the turkey reach room temperature
6. Preheat the air fryer to 175C
7. Cook for 15 minutes, ensuring the turkey is cooked through before serving

# Cheddar & Bbq Stuffed Chicken

Servings: 2

**Ingredients:**
- 3 strips of bacon
- 100g cheddar cheese
- 3 tbsp barbecue sauce
- 300g skinless and boneless chicken breasts
- salt and ground pepper to taste

**Directions:**
1. Preheat the air fryer to 190°C
2. Cook one of the back strips for 2 minutes, before cutting into small pieces
3. Increase the temperature of the air fryer to 200°C
4. Mix together the cooked bacon, cheddar cheese and 1 tbsp barbecue sauce
5. Take the chicken and make a pouch by cutting a 1 inch gap into the top
6. Stuff the pouch with the bacon and cheese mixture and then wrap around the chicken breast
7. Coat the chicken with the rest of the BBQ sauce
8. Cook for 10 minutes in the air fryer, before turning and cooking for an additional 10 minutes

# Air Fryer Chicken Breast

Servings: 2
Cooking Time: 10 Mints

**Ingredients:**
- 1 large egg, beaten
- 30 g plain flour
- 75 g panko bread crumbs
- 35 g freshly grated Parmesan
- 2 tsp. lemon zest
- 1 tsp. dried oregano
- 1/2 tsp. cayenne pepper
- Salt
- Freshly ground black pepper
- 2 boneless skinless chicken breasts

**Directions:**
1. Place eggs and flour in two separate shallow bowls. In a third shallow bowl, combine panko, Parmesan, lemon zest, oregano, and cayenne. Season with salt and pepper.
2. Working one at a time, dip chicken into flour, then eggs, and then panko mixture, pressing to coat.
3. Place in air fryer basket and cook at 190°C/375°F for 10 minutes. Flip chicken, and cook for another 5 minutes, until coating is golden and chicken is cooked through

# Bbq Chicken Tenders

Servings: 6

**Ingredients:**
- 300g barbecue flavoured pork rinds
- 200g all purpose flour
- 1 tbsp barbecue seasoning
- 1 egg
- 400g chicken breast tenderloins
- Cooking spray

**Directions:**
1. Preheat the air fryer to 190°C
2. Place the pork rinds into a food processor and blitz to a breadcrumb consistency, before transferring to a bowl
3. In a separate bowl, combine the flour and barbecue seasoning
4. Beat the egg in a small bowl
5. Take the chicken and first dip into the egg, then the flour, and then the breadcrumbs
6. Place the chicken into the air fryer and spray with cooking spray and cook for about 15 minutes

# Air Fryer Frozen Chicken Cordon Bleu

Servings: 1
Cooking Time: 15 Mints

**Ingredients:**
- 1 frozen chicken cordon bleu

**Directions:**
1. Preheat air fryer to 180°C/350°F, for approximately 2-3 minutes.
2. Place frozen chicken cordon bleu in an air fryer basket. If you are cooking more than one, ensure they are not touching.
3. Air fry cordon bleu for: 15-20 minutes for frozen pre-cooked cordon bleu, or - 30-35 minutes for frozen raw cordon bleu See note 2.
4. When cooking time is up, check internal temperature to make sure cordon bleu have reached at least 74°C/165°F in the center of the thickest part. If required, air fry for additional 2-3 minute intervals until the correct temperature is reached

# Buffalo Wings

Servings: 4

**Ingredients:**

- 500g chicken wings
- 1 tbsp olive oil
- 5 tbsp cayenne pepper sauce
- 75g butter
- 2 tbsp vinegar
- 1 tsp garlic powder
- ¼ tsp cayenne pepper

**Directions:**

1. Preheat the air fryer to 182C
2. Take a large mixing bowl and add the chicken wings
3. Drizzle oil over the wings, coating evenly
4. Cook for 25 minutes and then flip the wings and cook for 5 more minutes
5. In a saucepan over a medium heat, mix the hot pepper sauce, butter, vinegar, garlic powder and cayenne pepper, combining well
6. Pour the sauce over the wings and flip to coat, before serving

# Air Fryer Rotisserie Chicken

Servings: 6
Cooking Time: 20 Mints

**Ingredients:**

- 1.3kg chicken, cut into 8 pieces
- Salt
- Freshlyground black pepper
- 1 tbsp. dried thyme
- 2 tsp. dried oregano
- 2 tsp. garlic powder
- 2 tsp. onion powder
- 1 tsp. smoked paprika
- 1/4 tsp. cayenn

**Directions:**

1. Season chicken pieces all over with salt and pepper. In a medium bowl, whisk to combine herbs and spices, then rub spice mix all over chicken pieces.
2. Add dark meat pieces to air fryer basket and cook at 180°C/350°F for 10 minutes, then flip and cook 10 minutes more. Repeat with chicken breasts, but reduce time to 8 minutes per side. Use a meat thermometer to insure that chicken is cooked through, each piece should register 73°C/165°F.

# Air Fryer Chicken Parmesan

Servings: 4
Cooking Time: 10 Mints

**Ingredients:**

- 2 large boneless chicken breasts
- Salt
- Freshlyground black pepper
- 40 g plain flour
- 2 large eggs
- 100 g panko bread crumbs
- 25 g freshly grated Parmesan
- 1 tsp. dried oregano
- 1/2 tsp.
- garlic powder
- 1/2 tsp. chilli flakes
- 240 g marinara/tomato sauce
- 100 g grated mozzarella
- Freshly chopped parsley, for garnish

**Directions:**

1. Pat the skin of your chicken dry and using a knife make small holes all around the chicken.
2. In a blender combine all remaining ingredients and blend for three minutes. Pour half the jerk marinade over the chicken and massage it in. Refrigerate overnight.
3. When ready to cook, bring grill temperature up to 165°C/330°F. Place the chicken skin side down and close BBQ lid for 5-7 minutes until it starts to brown. Turn over and cook for the remaining 5-7 minutes. Repeat twice more until chicken is dark brown and cooked all the way through.
4. Move chicken to the sides of the grill and brush remaining jerk sauce on top. Close the lid and cook for a further 5-7minutes.
5. Remove from BBQ and leave chicken to cool for around 10 minutes. Either eat on the bone or chop the meat into smaller pieces and serve.

## Air Fryer Tikka Chicken Breast

Servings: 2
Cooking Time: 5 Mints
**Ingredients:**
- Chicken breasts
- 2 tablespoons of Tikka paste
- 1/4 tablespoon of olive oil or spray oil

**Directions:**
1. Coat chicken breasts in 1/4 tablespoon of olive oil mixed with the 2 tablespoons of Tikka paste.
2. Spray the air fryer basket with oil to prevent the chicken breasts from sticking.
3. Cook at 180°C/360°F for 8-9 minutes.
4. Turn the chicken breasts over and then cook for a further 8-9 minutes.
5. Check the internal temperature is at least 74°C/165°F before serving

## Air Fryer Chicken Wings With Honey And Sesame

Servings: 1-2
Cooking Time: 10-30 Mints
**Ingredients:**
- 450–500g /2 oz chicken wings with tips removed
- 1 tbsp olive oil
- 3 tbsp cornflour
- 1 tbsp runny honey
- 1 tsp soy sauceor tamari
- 1 tsp rice wine vinegar
- 1 tsp toasted sesame oil
- 2 tsp sesame seeds, toasted
- 1 large spring onion, thinly sliced
- salt and freshly ground black pepper

**Directions:**
1. In a large bowl, toss together the chicken wings, olive oil and a generous amount of salt and pepper. Toss in the cornflour, a tablespoon at a time, until the wings are well coated.
2. Air-fry the chicken wings in a single layer for 25 minutes at 180°C/350°F, turning halfway through the cooking time.
3. Meanwhile, make the glaze by whisking together the honey, soy sauce, rice wine vinegar and toasted sesame oil in a large bowl.
4. Tip the cooked wings into the glaze, tossing until they're well coated. Return to the air fryer in a single layer for 5 more minutes.
5. Toss the wings once more in any remaining glaze. Sprinkle with toasted sesame seeds and spring onion and serve.

# Air Fryer Chicken Tenders

Servings: 4
Cooking Time: 15 Mints

**Ingredients:**

- 675 g chicken tenders
- Salt
- Freshly ground black pepper
- 195 g plain flour
- 250 g panko bread crumbs
- 2 large eggs
- 60 ml buttermilk
- Cooking spray
- FOR THE HONEY MUSTARD
- 3 tbsp. honey
- 2 tbsp. dijon mustard
- 1/4 tsp. hot sauce (optional)
- Pinch of salt
- 80 g mayonnaise
- Freshlyground black pepper

**Directions:**

1. Season chicken tenders on both sides with salt and pepper. Place flour and bread crumbs in two separate shallow bowls. In a third bowl, whisk together eggs and buttermilk. Working one at a time, dip chicken in flour, then egg mixture, and finally in bread crumbs, pressing to coat.
2. Working in batches, place chicken tenders in basket of air fryer, being sure to not overcrowd it. Spray the tops of chicken with cooking spray and cook at 200°C/400°F for 5 minutes. Flip chicken over, spray the tops with more cooking spray and cook 5 minutes more. Repeat with remaining chicken tenders.
3. Make sauce: In a small bowl, whisk together mayonnaise, honey, dijon, and hot sauce, if using. Season with a pinch of salt and a few cracks of black pepper.
4. Serve chicken tenders with honey mustard

# Chapter 5 Beef & Lamb And Pork Recipes

## Steak Popcorn Bites

Servings: 4

**Ingredients:**

- 500g steak, cut into 1" sized cubes
- 500g potato chips, ridged ones work best
- 100g flour
- 2 beaten eggs
- Salt and pepper to taste

**Directions:**

1. Place the chips into the food processor and pulse unit you get fine chip crumbs
2. Take a bowl and combine the flour with salt and pepper
3. Add the chips to another bowl and the beaten egg to another bowl
4. Take the steak cubes and dip first in the flour, then the egg and then the chip crumbs
5. Preheat your air fryer to 260ºC
6. Place the steak pieces into the fryer and cook for 9 minutes

## Chinese Pork With Pineapple

Servings: 4

**Ingredients:**

- 450g pork loin, cubed
- ½ tsp salt
- ½ tsp pepper
- 1 tbsp brown sugar
- 75g fresh coriander, chopped
- 2 tbsp toasted sesame seeds
- ½ pineapple, cubed
- 1 sliced red pepper
- 1 minced clove of garlic
- 1 tsp ginger
- 2 tbsp soy
- 1 tbsp oil

**Directions:**

1. Season the pork with salt and pepper
2. Add all ingredients to the air fryer
3. Cook at 180ºC for 17 minutes
4. Serve and garnish with coriander and toasted sesame seeds

# **Simple Steaks**

Servings: 2
Cooking Time: X
**Ingredients:**
- 2 x 220-g/8-oz. sirloin steaks
- 2 teaspoons olive oil
- salt and freshly ground black pepper

**Directions:**
1. Bring the steaks out of the fridge an hour before cooking. Drizzle with the oil, then rub with salt and pepper on both sides. Leave to marinate at room temperature for 1 hour.
2. Preheat the air-fryer to 180°C/350°F.
3. Add the steaks to the preheated air-fryer and air-fry for 5 minutes on one side, then turn and cook for a further 4 minutes on the other side (for medium rare). Check the internal temperature of the steak has reached 58°C/135°F using a meat thermometer – if not, cook for another few minutes. Leave to rest for a few minutes before serving.

# **Air Fryer Rack Of Lamb**

Servings: 2
Cooking Time: 15 Mints
**Ingredients:**
- 397 g/14 oz lamb rack
- 1 tbsp olive oil
- 1 tsp rosemary, fresh or dried
- 1 tsp thyme, fresh or dried
- ½ tsp salt
- ½ tsp black pepper

**Directions:**
1. Preheat air fryer to 360°F (180°C)
2. Mix olive oil with rosemary, thyme, salt and pepper on a large plate.
3. Pat lamb rack dry and press into the herb oil mixture, flip it over and rub the herb mix in so the lamb is well coated.
4. Place lamb rack in air fryer basket, and air fry for 15-20 minutes for medium done lamb.
5. Check the temperature with a meat thermometer to ensure that it is cooked to your liking (medium should be 130-135°F /54–57°C). Cook for additional 3 minute intervals if you prefer it more well done.
6. Remove lamb rack from air fryer, cover with kitchen foil and leave to rest for at least five minutes before serving.

# Beef Stirfry

Servings: 2

**Ingredients:**
- 500g steak
- 400g broccoli
- 3 peppers, cut into strips
- 1 tbsp ground ginger
- 25ml water
- 1 sliced onion
- 25g hoisin sauce
- 2 tsp minced garlic
- 1 tsp sesame oil
- 1 tbsp soy

**Directions:**
1. Add sesame oil, hoisin sauce, garlic, soy and water to a bowl and then add the steak, allow to marinate for 20 minutes
2. Mix 1 tbsp of oil with the vegetables and place in the air fryer, cook at 200°C for about 5 minutes
3. Place the vegetables in a bowl and put aside
4. Add meat to air fryer and cook for 4 minutes, turn and cook for a further 2 minutes
5. Mix the steak with the vegetables and serve with rice

# Air Fryer Lamb Steaks

Servings: 2
Cooking Time: 7 Mints

**Ingredients:**
- 2 lamb steaks
- ½ teaspoon ground black pepper
- ½ teaspoon kosher salt
- Drizzle of light olive oil

**Directions:**
1. Remove steak from the refrigerator an hour before cooking to allow it to reach room temperature before cooking.
2. Preheat air fryer to 400°F/200°C.
3. Mix salt and ground pepper on a plate.
4. Pat lamb steaks dry, then rub or spray with a little olive oil.
5. Press each side of the steak into the salt/pepper mix, then place in air fryer basket. ensure they are not touching.
6. Air fry lamb steaks for 5 minutes for medium-rare (9 minutes for well-done).
7. Use an instant-read meat thermometer to check the internal temperature - it should be 160°F/71°C for medium-rare, or 170°F/76°C or above for well done. Remove lamb steaks from the air fryer, cover with foil and leave to rest for 5 minutes before serving.

# Italian Meatballs

Servings: 12
**Ingredients:**
- 2 tbsp olive oil
- 2 tbsp minced shallot
- 3 cloves garlic minced
- 100g panko crumbs
- 35g chopped parsley
- 1 tbsp chopped rosemary
- 60ml milk
- 400g minced pork
- 250g turkey sausage
- 1 egg beaten
- 1 tbsp dijon mustard
- 1 tbsp finely chopped thyme

**Directions:**
1. Preheat air fryer to 200ºC
2. Heat oil in a pan and cook the garlic and shallot over a medium heat for 1-2 minutes
3. Mix the panko and milk in a bowl and allow to stand for 5 minutes
4. Add all the ingredients to the panko mix and combine well
5. Shape into 1 ½ inch meatballs and cook for 12 minutes

# Sticky Asian Beef

Servings: 2
**Ingredients:**
- 1 tbsp coconut oil
- 2 sliced peppers
- 25g liquid aminos
- 25g cup water
- 100g brown sugar
- ¼ tsp pepper
- ½ tsp ground ginger
- ½ tbsp minced garlic
- 1 tsp red pepper flakes
- 600g steak thinly sliced
- ¼ tsp salt

**Directions:**
1. Melt the coconut oil in a pan, add the peppers and cook until softened
2. In another pan add the aminos, brown sugar, ginger, garlic and pepper flakes. Mix and bring to the boil, simmer for 10 mins
3. Season the steak with salt and pepper
4. Put the steak in the air fryer and cook at 200ºC for 10 minutes. Turn the steak and cook for a further 5 minutes until crispy
5. Add the steak to the peppers then mix with the sauce
6. Serve with rice

# Pork Chops With Sprouts

Servings: 2

**Ingredients:**
- 300g pork chops
- ⅛ tsp salt
- ½ tsp pepper
- 250g Brussels sprouts quartered
- 1 tsp olive oil
- 1 tsp maple syrup
- 1 tsp dijon mustard

**Directions:**
1. Season the pork chops with salt and pepper
2. Mix together oil, maple syrup and mustard. Add Brussels sprouts
3. Add pork chops and Brussels sprouts to the air fryer and cook at 200°C for about 10 minutes

# Apricot Lamb Burgers

Servings: 4
Cooking Time: X

**Ingredients:**
- 500 g/1 lb. 2 oz. minced/ground lamb
- 50 g/⅓ cup dried apricots, finely chopped
- 1 teaspoon ground cumin
- ½ teaspoon ground coriander
- ¾ teaspoon salt
- 1 egg, beaten

**Directions:**
1. Combine all the ingredients together in a food processor, then divide into 4 equal portions and mould into burgers.
2. Preheat the air-fryer to 180°C/350°F.
3. Add the burgers to the preheated air-fryer and air-fry for 15 minutes, turning carefully halfway through cooking. Check the internal temperature of the burgers has reached 75°C/170°F using a meat thermometer – if not, cook for another few minutes and then serve.

## Pork With Chinese 5 Spice

Servings: 4

**Ingredients:**

- 2 pork rounds cut into chunks
- 2 large eggs
- 1 tsp sesame oil
- 200g cornstarch
- 1/4 tsp salt
- ½ tsp pepper
- 3 tbsp canola oil
- 1 tsp Chinese 5 spice

**Directions:**

1. In a bowl mix the corn starch, salt, pepper and 5 spice
2. Mix the eggs and sesame oil in another bowl
3. Dip the pork into the egg and then cover in the corn starch mix
4. Place in the air fryer and cook at 170ºC for 11-12 minutes, shaking halfway through
5. Serve with sweet and sour sauce

## Mini Moroccan Lamb Burgers

Servings: 2
Cooking Time: X

**Ingredients:**

- 400 g/14 oz. minced/ground lamb
- 1 tablespoon freshly chopped coriander/cilantro
- 1 teaspoon freshly chopped mint
- ½ teaspoon smoked paprika
- 1 teaspoon ground cumin
- 1 tablespoon harissa paste
- tzatziki , to serve
- pitta breads and salad leaves, to serve

**Directions:**

1. Combine all the ingredients in a food processor, then divide into 6 equal portions and mould into burgers.
2. Preheat the air-fryer to 180ºC/350ºF.
3. Add the burgers to the preheated air-fryer and air-fry for 9 minutes, turning halfway through cooking. Check the internal temperature of the burgers has reached at least 75ºC/170ºF using a meat thermometer – if not, cook for another few minutes. Serve tucked into warmed pitta breads, with salad leaves and tzatziki.

# Mongolian Beef

Servings: 4

**Ingredients:**
- 500g steak
- 25g cornstarch
- 2 tsp vegetable oil
- ½ tsp ginger
- 1 tbsp garlic minced
- 75g soy sauce
- 75g water
- 100g brown sugar

**Directions:**
1. Slice the steak and coat in corn starch
2. Place in the air fryer and cook at 200°C for 10 minutes turning halfway
3. Place remaining ingredients in a sauce pan and gently warm
4. When cooked place the steak in a bowl and pour the sauce over

# Salt And Pepper Belly Pork

Servings: 4

**Ingredients:**
- 500g belly pork
- 1 tsp pepper
- ½ tsp salt

**Directions:**
1. Cut the pork into bite size pieces and season with salt and pepper
2. Heat the air fryer to 200°C
3. Place in the air fryer and cook for 15 minutes until crisp

# Traditional Empanadas

Servings: 2

**Ingredients:**

- 300g minced beef
- 1 tbsp olive oil
- ¼ cup finely chopped onion
- 150g chopped mushrooms
- ⅛ tsp cinnamon
- 4 chopped tomatoes
- 2 tsp chopped garlic
- 6 green olives
- ¼ tsp paprika
- ¼ tsp cumin
- 8 goyoza wrappers
- 1 beaten egg

**Directions:**

1. Heat oil in a pan add onion and minced beef and cook until browned
2. Add mushrooms and cook for 6 minutes
3. Add garlic, olives, paprika, cumin and cinnamon, and cook for about 3 minutes
4. Stir in tomatoes and cook for 1 minute, set aside allow to cool
5. Place 1 ½ tbsp of filling in each goyoza wrapper
6. Brush edges with egg fold over and seal pinching edges
7. Place in the air fryer and cook at 200 for about 7 minutes

# Air Fryer Bacon-wrapped Asparagus

Servings: 4
Cooking Time: 10 Mints

**Ingredients:**

- 12 asparagus spears
- 12 slices bacon
- 1 tablespoon light olive oil

**Directions:**

1. Preheat air fryer to 200°C/400°F.
2. Trim any woody bits from the ends of the asparagus spears, then wrap each asparagus spear with bacon, wrapping tightly from the bottom towards the top.
3. Lightly brush or spritz the air fryer basket with oil (optional, but recommended if your air fryer is prone to sticking). Then place the bacon wrapped asparagus in the air fryer in a single layer. Try to ensure it is not touching.
4. Air fry the asparagus for 10-15 minutes flipping it over halfway through the cooking time if required for your air fryer.
5. Cook until the bacon is crispy.

# Pulled Pork, Bacon, And Cheese Sliders

Servings: 2
Cooking Time: 30 Minutes

**Ingredients:**
- 2 x 50 g / 3.5 oz pork steaks
- 1 tsp salt
- 1 tsp black pepper
- 4 slices bacon strips, chopped into small pieces
- 1 tbsp soy sauce
- 1 tbsp BBQ sauce
- 100 g / 7 oz cheddar cheese, grated
- 2 bread buns

**Directions:**
1. Preheat the air fryer to 200 °C / 400 °F and line the bottom of the basket with parchment paper.
2. Place the pork steaks on a clean surface and season with salt and black pepper. Move the pork steak in the prepared air fryer basket and cook for 15 minutes.
3. Remove the steak from the air fryer and shred using two forks. Mix with the chopped bacon in a heatproof bowl and place the bowl in the air fryer. Cook for 10 minutes.
4. Remove the bowl from the air fryer and stir in the soy sauce and BBQ sauce. Return the bowl to the air fryer basket and continue cooking for a further 5 minutes.
5. Meanwhile, spread the cheese across one half of the bread buns. Top with the cooked pulled pork and an extra squirt of BBQ sauce.

# Honey & Mustard Meatballs

Servings: 4

**Ingredients:**
- 500g minced pork
- 1 red onion
- 1 tsp mustard
- 2 tsp honey
- 1 tsp garlic puree
- 1 tsp pork seasoning
- Salt and pepper

**Directions:**
1. Thinly slice the onion
2. Place all the ingredients in a bowl and mix until well combined
3. Form into meatballs, place in the air fryer and cook at 180°C for 10 minutes

# Lamb Koftas

Servings: 3
Cooking Time: X

**Ingredients:**
- 600 g/1 lb. 5 oz. minced/ground lamb
- 1 onion, finely chopped
- 1 garlic clove, finely chopped
- 2 tablespoons finely chopped coriander/cilantro
- 1 teaspoon ground coriander
- 1 teaspoon ground cumin
- 1 teaspoon ground turmeric
- ½ teaspoon chilli/chili powder
- 1 teaspoon dried thyme
- 1 teaspoon salt
- 1 tablespoon runny honey

**Directions:**
1. Combine all the ingredients in a bowl and mix together well. Divide into 6 equal portions and mould into sausage shapes. Place in the fridge for at least an hour before cooking.
2. Preheat the air-fryer to 180°C/350°F.
3. Thread a small metal skewer through each kofta. Place in the preheated air-fryer and air-fry for 10 minutes, turning halfway through cooking. Check the internal temperature of the koftas has reached at least 70°C/160°F using a meat thermometer – if not, cook for another few minutes and then serve.

# Beef Nacho Pinwheels

Servings: 6

**Ingredients:**
- 500g minced beef
- 1 packet of taco seasoning
- 300ml water
- 300ml sour cream
- 6 tostadas
- 6 flour tortillas
- 3 tomatoes
- 250g nacho cheese
- 250g shredded lettuce
- 250g Mexican cheese

**Directions:**
1. Preheat air fryer to 200°C
2. Brown the mince in a pan and add the taco seasoning
3. Share the remaining ingredients between the tortillas
4. Fold the edges of the tortillas up towards the centre, should look like a pinwheel
5. Lay seam down in the air fryer and cook for 2 minutes
6. Turnover and cook for a further 2 minutes

# Chapter 6 Fish & Seafood Recipes

## Air Fryer Spicy Bay Scallops

Servings: 4
Cooking Time: 10 Mints

**Ingredients:**
- 454 g bay scallops, rinsed and patted dry
- 2 teaspoons smoked paprika
- 2 teaspoons chili powder
- 2 teaspoons olive oil
- 1 teaspoon garlic powder
- ¼ teaspoon ground black pepper
- ⅛ teaspoon cayenne red pepper

**Directions:**
1. Preheat an air fryer to 400°F/200°C.
2. Combine bay scallops, smoked paprika, chili powder, olive oil, garlic powder, pepper, and cayenne pepper in a bowl; stir until evenly combined. Transfer to the air fryer basket.
3. Air fry until scallops are cooked through, about 8 minutes, shaking basket halfway through the cooking time.

## Lemon Pepper Shrimp

Servings: 2

**Ingredients:**
- ½ tbsp olive oil
- The juice of 1 lemon
- ¼ tsp paprika
- 1 tsp lemon pepper
- ¼ tsp garlic powder
- 400g uncooked shrimp
- 1 sliced lemon

**Directions:**
1. Preheat air fryer to 200°C
2. Mix olive oil, lemon juice, paprika, lemon pepper and garlic powder. Add the shrimp and mix well
3. Place shrimp in the air fryer and cook for 6-8 minutes until pink and firm.
4. Serve with lemon slices

# Air Fryer Orange Shrimp & Broccol

Servings: 3-4
Cooking Time: 20 Mints

**Ingredients:**

- 1 box Popcorn Shrimp
- 1 large or 2 small heads broccoli
- 1 tbsp olive oil
- 1/2 tsp salt
- 1/4 tsp pepper
- 85 ml orange juice
- 2 tbsp honey
- 2 tbsp soy sauce or coconut aminos
- 1 tsp minced garlic
- 1 tsp minced ginger
- 1 tsp sriracha or chili garlic sauce
- 1 tbsp cornstarch or arrowroot powder

**Directions:**

1. Toss broccoli crowns with olive oil, salt and pepper. Add to air fryer basket and air fry for 6 minutes at 200°C/400°F.
2. Remove broccoli from air fryer.
3. Cook the half of the bag of the Popcorn Shrimp in your air fryer at 200°C/400°F for 8 – 10 minutes, until reaching an internal temperature of 165°C/320°F or higher.
4. Make sauce by whisking together orange juice, honey, soy sauce, garlic, ginger, sriracha and cornstarch. Heat over low heat for 10-15 minutes, whisking occasionally until sauce thickens and becomes sticky.
5. Toss shrimp in about half the sauce to start. Add broccoli and toss to combine.
6. Serve with rice and the remaining sauce to dip or drizzle on top. Enjoy

# Pesto Salmon

Servings: 4

**Ingredients:**

- 4 x 150–175-g/5½–6-oz. salmon fillets
- lemon wedges, to serve
- PESTO
- 50 g/scant ½ cup toasted pine nuts
- 50 g/2 oz. fresh basil
- 50 g/⅔ cup grated Parmesan or Pecorino
- 100 ml/7 tablespoons olive oil

**Directions:**

1. To make the pesto, blitz the pine nuts, basil and Parmesan to a paste in a food processor. Pour in the olive oil and process again.
2. Preheat the air-fryer to 160ºC/325ºF.
3. Top each salmon fillet with 2 tablespoons of the pesto. Add the salmon fillets to the preheated air-fryer and air-fry for 9 minutes. Check the internal temperature of the fish has reached at least 63ºC/145ºF using a meat thermometer – if not, cook for another few minutes.

# Shrimp With Yum Yum Sauce

Servings: 4

**Ingredients:**
- 400g peeled jumbo shrimp
- 1 tbsp soy sauce
- 1 tbsp garlic paste
- 1 tbsp ginger paste
- 4 tbsp mayo
- 2 tbsp ketchup
- 1 tbsp sugar
- 1 tsp paprika
- 1 tsp garlic powder

**Directions:**
1. Mix soy sauce, garlic paste and ginger paste in a bowl. Add the shrimp, allow to marinate for 15 minutes
2. In another bowl mix ketchup, mayo, sugar, paprika and the garlic powder to make the yum yum sauce.
3. Set the air fryer to 200°C, place shrimp in the basket and cook for 8-10 minutes

# Fish In Foil

Servings: 2

**Ingredients:**
- 1 tablespoon avocado oil or olive oil, plus extra for greasing
- 1 tablespoon soy sauce (or tamari)
- 1½ teaspoons freshly grated garlic
- 1½ teaspoons freshly grated ginger
- 1 small red chilli/chile, finely chopped
- 2 skinless, boneless white fish fillets (about 350 g/12 oz. total weight)

**Directions:**
1. Mix the oil, soy sauce, garlic, ginger and chilli/chile together. Brush a little oil onto two pieces of foil, then lay the fish in the centre of the foil. Spoon the topping mixture over the fish. Wrap the foil around the fish to make a parcel, with a gap above the fish but shallow enough to fit in your air-fryer basket.
2. Preheat the air-fryer to 180°C/350°F.
3. Add the foil parcels to the preheated air-fryer and air-fry for 7–10 minutes, depending on the thickness of your fillets. The fish should just flake when a fork is inserted. Serve immediately.

# Coconut Shrimp

Servings: 4

**Ingredients:**
- 250g flour
- 1 ½ tsp black pepper
- 2 eggs
- 150g unsweetened flaked coconut
- 1 Serrano chilli, thinly sliced
- 25g panko bread crumbs
- 300g shrimp raw
- ½ tsp salt
- 4 tbsp honey
- 25ml lime juice

**Directions:**
1. Mix together flour and pepper, in another bowl beat the eggs and in another bowl mix the panko and coconut
2. Dip each of the shrimp in the flour mix then the egg and then cover in the coconut mix
3. Coat the shrimp in cooking spray
4. Place in the air fryer and cook at 200°C for 6-8 mins turning half way through
5. Mix together the honey, lime juice and chilli and serve with the shrimp

# Copycat Fish Fingers

Servings: 2

**Ingredients:**
- 2 slices wholemeal bread, grated into breadcrumbs
- 50g plain flour
- 1 beaten egg
- 1 white fish fillet
- The juice of 1 small lemon
- 1 tsp parsley
- 1 tsp thyme
- 1 tsp mixed herbs
- Salt and pepper to taste

**Directions:**
1. Preheat the air fryer to 180°C
2. Add salt pepper and parsley to the breadcrumbs and combine well
3. Place the egg in another bowl
4. Place the flour in a separate bowl
5. Place the fish into a food processor and add the lemon juice, salt, pepper thyme and mixed herbs
6. Blitz to create a crumb-like consistency
7. Roll your fish in the flour, then the egg and then the breadcrumbs
8. Cook at 180°C for 8 minutes

# Air Fryer Crab Cakes

Servings: 6
Cooking Time: 5 Mins

**Ingredients:**
- 60 g mayonnaise
- 1 egg
- 2 tbsp. chives, finely chopped
- 2 tsp. Dijon mustard
- 2 tsp. cajun seasoning
- 1 tsp. lemon zest
- 1/2 tsp. salt
- 450 g jumbo lump crab meat
- 120 g Cracker crumbs (from about 20 crackers)
- Cooking spray
- Hot sauce, for serving
- Lemon wedges, for serving
- FOR THE TARTAR SAUCE
- 60 g mayonnaise
- 80 1/2 g dill pickle, finely chopped
- 1 tbsp. shallot, finely chopped
- 2 tsp. capers, finely chopped
- 1 tsp. fresh lemon juice
- 1/4 tsp. Dijon mustard
- 1 tsp. fresh dill, finely chopped

**Directions:**
1. Make crab cakes: In a large bowl, whisk together mayo, egg, chives, Dijon mustard, cajun seasoning, lemon zest and salt. Fold in the crab meat and the cracker crumbs.
2. Divide the mixture equally, forming 8 patties. You can refrigerate them for up to 4 hours if you're not ready to fry them. (Patties can also be frozen on a parchment-lined baking tray.)
3. Heat the air fryer to 190°C/375°F and spray the basket and the tops of the crab cakes with cooking spray. Place the crab cakes into the basket in a single layer. Cook until deep golden brown and crisp, about 12-14 minutes, flipping halfway through.
4. Meanwhile, make tartar sauce: Combine all of the tartar sauce ingredients in a bowl.
5. Serve the crab cakes warm with hot sauce, lemon wedges, and tartar sauce.

# Peppery Lemon Shrimp

Servings: 2

**Ingredients:**
- 300g uncooked shrimp
- 1 tbsp olive oil
- 1 the juice of 1 lemon
- 0.25 tsp garlic powder
- 1 sliced lemon
- 1 tsp pepper
- 0.25 tsp paprika

**Directions:**
1. Heat the fryer to 200ºC
2. Take a medium sized mixing bowl and combine the lemon juice, pepper, garlic powder, paprika and the olive oil together
3. Add the shrimp to the bowl and make sure they're well coated
4. Arrange the shrimp into the basket of the fryer
5. Cook for between 6-8 minutes, until firm and pink

# Cod In Parma Ham

Servings: 2

**Ingredients:**
- 2 x 175–190-g/6–7-oz. cod fillets, skin removed
- 6 slices Parma ham or prosciutto
- 16 cherry tomatoes
- 60 g/2 oz. rocket/arugula
- DRESSING
- 1 tablespoon olive oil
- 1½ teaspoons balsamic vinegar
- garlic salt, to taste
- freshly ground black pepper, to taste

**Directions:**
1. Preheat the air-fryer to 180ºC/350ºF.
2. Wrap each piece of cod snugly in 3 ham slices. Add the ham-wrapped cod fillets and the tomatoes to the preheated air-fryer and air-fry for 6 minutes, turning the cod halfway through cooking. Check the internal temperature of the fish has reached at least 60ºC/140ºF using a meat thermometer – if not, cook for another minute.
3. Meanwhile, make the dressing by combining all the ingredients in a jar and shaking well.
4. Serve the cod and tomatoes on a bed of rocket/arugula with the dressing poured over.

# Garlic Butter Salmon

Servings: 2

**Ingredients:**
- 2 salmon fillets, boneless with the skin left on
- 1 tsp minced garlic
- 2 tbsp melted butter
- 1 tsp chopped parsley
- Salt and pepper to taste

**Directions:**
1. Preheat the air fryer to 270 ºC
2. Take a bowl and combine the melted butter, parsley and garlic to create a sauce
3. Season the salmon to your liking
4. Brush the salmon with the garlic mixture, on both sides
5. Place the salmon into the fryer, with the skin side facing down
6. Cook for 10 minutes - the salmon is done when it flakes with ease

# Air Fryer Lemon Pepper Shrimp

Servings: 2

Cooking Time: 15 Mints

**Ingredients:**
- 1 tablespoon olive oil
- 1 lemon, juiced
- 1 teaspoon lemon pepper
- ¼ teaspoon paprika
- ¼ teaspoon garlic powder
- 340 g uncooked medium shrimp, peeled and deveined
- 1 lemon, sliced

**Directions:**
1. Preheat an air fryer to 400°F 200°C according to the manufacturer's instructions.
2. Combine oil, lemon juice, lemon pepper, paprika, and garlic powder in a bowl. Add shrimp and toss to coat.
3. Cook shrimp in the preheated air fryer until they are bright pink on the outside and the meat is opaque, about 6 to 8 minutes. Serve with lemon slices.

# Fish Sticks With Tartar Sauce Batter

Servings: 4

**Ingredients:**
- 6 tbsp mayonnaise
- 2 tbsp dill pickle
- 1 tsp seafood seasoning
- 400g cod fillets, cut into sticks
- 300g panko breadcrumbs

**Directions:**
1. Combine the mayonnaise, seafood seasoning and dill pickle in a large bowl.
2. Add the cod sticks and coat well
3. Preheat air fryer to 200ºC
4. Coat the fish sticks in the breadcrumbs
5. Place in the air fryer and cook for 12 minutes

# Air Fryer Fish Fillets

Servings: 3
Cooking Time: 15 Mints

**Ingredients:**
- 1 pound (454 g) white fish fillets (cod, halibut, tilapia, etc.)
- 1 teaspoon (5 ml) kosher salt , or to taste
- 1/2 teaspoon (2.5 ml) black pepper , or to taste
- 1 teaspoon (5 ml) garlic powder
- 1 teaspoon (5 ml) paprika
- 1-2 cups (60-120 g) breading of choice breadcrumbs, panko, crushed pork rinds or almond flour
- 1 egg , or more if needed

**Directions:**
1. Preheat the Air Fryer at 380°F/193°C for 4 minutes.
2. Cut fish filets in half if needed. Make sure they are even sized so they'll cook evenly.
3. Pat the filets dry. Lightly oil the filets and then season with salt, black pepper, garlic powder, and paprika.
4. Put the breading in a shallow bowl. In another bowl, beat the eggs. Dip the filets in the egg, shaking off excess egg. Dredge the filets in your breading of choice. Press filets into the bowl of breading so that they completely coat the filets. Repeat this process for all fish pieces.
5. Lightly spray parchment paper with oil spray. Lay coated fish in a single layer on parchment (cook in batches if needed). Generously spray all sides of the breaded filets with oil spray to coat any dry spots.
6. Air Fry at 380°F/193°C for 8-14 minutes, depending on the size and thickness of your filets. After 6 minutes, flip the filets. Lightly spray any dry spots than then continue cooking for the remaining time or until they are crispy brown and the fish is cooked through. Serve with your favorite dip: tartar sauce, mustard, aioli, etc

# Air Fryer Tuna

Servings: 2

**Ingredients:**
- 2 tuna steaks, boneless and skinless
- 2 tsp honey
- 1 tsp grated ginger
- 4 tbsp soy sauce
- 1 tsp sesame oil
- 1/2 tsp rice vinegar

**Directions:**
1. Combine the honey, soy sauce, rice vinegar and sesame oil in a bowl until totally mixed together
2. Cover the tuna steaks with the sauce and place in the refrigerator for half an hour to marinade
3. Preheat the air fryer to 270°C
4. Cook the tuna for 4 minutes
5. Allow to rest before slicing

# Oat & Parmesan Crusted Fish Fillets

Servings: 2

**Ingredients:**
- 20 g/⅓ cup fresh breadcrumbs
- 25 g/3 tablespoons oats
- 15 g/¼ cup grated Parmesan
- 1 egg
- 2 x 175-g/6-oz. white fish fillets, skin-on
- salt and freshly ground black pepper

**Directions:**
1. Preheat the air-fryer to 180°C/350°F.
2. Combine the breadcrumbs, oats and cheese in a bowl and stir in a pinch of salt and pepper. In another bowl beat the egg. Dip the fish fillets in the egg, then top with the oat mixture.
3. Add the fish fillets to the preheated air-fryer on an air-fryer liner or a piece of pierced parchment paper. Air-fry for 10 minutes. Check the fish is just flaking away when a fork is inserted, then serve immediately.

# Salmon Patties

Servings: 4

**Ingredients:**

- 400g salmon
- 1 egg
- 1 diced onion
- 200g breadcrumbs
- 1 tsp dill weed

**Directions:**

1. Remove all bones and skin from the salmon
2. Mix egg, onion, dill weed and bread crumbs with the salmon
3. Shape mixture into patties and place into the air fryer
4. Set air fryer to 180°C
5. Cook for 5 minutes then turn them over and cook for a further 5 minutes until golden brown

# Store-cupboard Fishcakes

Servings: 3

**Ingredients:**

- 400 g/14 oz. cooked potato – either mashed potato or the insides of jacket potatoes (see page 124)
- 2 x 150–200-g/5½–7-oz. cans fish, such as tuna or salmon, drained
- 2 eggs
- ¾ teaspoon salt
- 1 teaspoon dried parsley
- ½ teaspoon freshly ground black pepper
- 1 tablespoon olive oil
- caper dressing (see page 79), to serve

**Directions:**

1. Mix the cooked potato, fish, eggs, salt, parsley and pepper together in a bowl, then divide into 6 equal portions and form into fishcakes. Drizzle the olive oil over both sides of each fishcake.
2. Preheat the air-fryer to 180°C/350°F.
3. Add the fishcakes to the preheated air-fryer and air-fry for 15 minutes, turning halfway through cooking. Serve with salad and tartare sauce or Caper Dressing.

## **Gluten Free Honey And Garlic Shrimp**

Servings: 2

**Ingredients:**
- 500g fresh shrimp
- 5 tbsp honey
- 2 tbsp gluten free soy sauce
- 2 tbsp tomato ketchup
- 250g frozen stir fry vegetables
- 1 crushed garlic clove
- 1 tsp fresh ginger
- 2 tbsp cornstarch

**Directions:**
1. Simmer the honey, soy sauce, garlic, tomato ketchup and ginger in a saucepan
2. Add the cornstarch and whisk until sauce thickens
3. Coat the shrimp with the sauce
4. Line the air fryer with foil and add the shrimp and vegetables
5. Cook at 180°C for 10 minutes

# Chapter 7 Vegetarian & Vegan Recipes

## **Lentil Burgers**

Servings: 4

**Ingredients:**
- 100g black buluga lentils
- 1 carrot, grated
- 1 diced onion
- 100g white cabbage
- 300g oats
- 1 tbsp garlic puree
- 1 tsp cumin
- Salt and pepper

**Directions:**
1. Blend the oats until they resemble flour
2. Put the lentils in a pan with water and cook for 45 minutes
3. Steam your vegetables for 5 minutes
4. Add all the ingredients into a bowl and mix well to combine
5. Form into burgers place in the air fryer and cook at 180°C for 30 minutes

# Paneer Tikka

Servings: 2

**Ingredients:**
- 200ml yogurt
- 1 tsp ginger garlic paste
- 1 tsp red chilli powder
- 1 tsp garam masala
- 1 tsp turmeric powder
- 1 tbsp dried fenugreek leaves
- The juice of 1 lemon
- 2 tbsp chopped coriander
- 1 tbsp olive oil
- 250g paneer cheese, cut into cubes
- 1 green pepper, chopped
- 1 red pepper, chopped
- 1 yellow pepper, chopped
- 1 chopped onion

**Directions:**
1. Take a mixing bowl and add the yogurt, garlic paste, red chilli powder, garam masala, turmeric powder, lemon juice, fenugreek and chopped coriander, combining well
2. Place the marinade to one side
3. Add the cubed cheese to the marinade and toss to coat well
4. Leave to marinade for 2 hours
5. Take 8 skewers and alternate the cheese with the peppers and onions
6. Drizzle a little oil over the top
7. Arrange in the air fryer and cook at 220ºC for 3 minutes
8. Turn and cook for another 3 minutes

# Rainbow Vegetables

Servings: 4

**Ingredients:**
- 1 red pepper, cut into slices
- 1 squash sliced
- 1 courgette sliced
- 1 tbsp olive oil
- 150g sliced mushrooms
- 1 onion sliced
- Salt and pepper to taste

**Directions:**
1. Preheat air fryer to 180ºC
2. Place all ingredients in a bowl and mix well
3. Place in the air fryer and cook for about 20 minutes turning halfway

# Orange Zingy Cauliflower

Servings: 2

**Ingredients:**

- 200ml water
- 200g flour
- Half the head of a cauliflower, cut into 1.5" florets
- 2 tsp olive oil
- 2 minced garlic cloves
- 1 tsp minced ginger
- 150ml orange juice
- 3 tbsp white vinegar
- 1/2 tsp red pepper flakes
- 1 tsp sesame oil 100g brown sugar
- 3 tbsp soy sauce
- 1 tbsp cornstarch
- 2 tbsp water
- 1 tsp salt

**Directions:**

1. Take a medium mixing bowl and add the water, salt and flour together
2. Dip each floret of cauliflower into the mixture and place in the air fryer basket
3. Cook at 220°C for 15 minutes
4. Meanwhile make the orange sauce by combining all ingredients in a saucepan and allowing to simmer for 3 minutes, until the sauce has thickened
5. Drizzle the sauce over the cauliflower to serve

# Spinach And Feta Croissants

Servings: 4

Cooking Time: 10 Minutes

**Ingredients:**

- 4 pre-made croissants
- 100 g / 7 oz feta cheese, crumbled
- 1 tsp dried chives
- 1 tsp garlic powder
- 50 g / 3.5 oz fresh spinach, chopped

**Directions:**

1. Preheat the air fryer to 180 °C / 350 °F. Remove the mesh basket from the air fryer machine and line with parchment paper.
2. Cut the croissants in half and lay each half out on the lined mesh basket.
3. In a bowl, combine the crumbled feta cheese, dried chives, garlic powder, and chopped spinach until they form a consistent mixture.
4. Spoon some of the mixture one half of the four croissants and cover with the second half of the croissants to seal in the filling.
5. Carefully slide the croissants in the mesh basket into the air fryer machine, close the lid, and cook for 10 minutes until the pastry is crispy and the feta cheese has melted.

# Air Feyer Breaded Asparagus Fries

Servings: 2
Cooking Time: 10 Mints

**Ingredients:**

- 227 g fresh asparagus, ends trimmed
- 1 egg, beaten
- 1/4 teaspoon salt, or to taste
- black pepper, to taste
- 1/2 teaspoon garlic powder, or to taste
- 27 g bread crumbs (Italian style or Japanese panko)
- 2 Tablespoons grated parmesan cheese
- Oil spray, for coating asparagus fries

**Directions:**

1. Pre-heat air fryer at 380°F/193°C for 5 minutes.
2. Trim the tough bottom ends of the asparagus (usually about the bottom 1-2 inches).
3. Lay the asparagus out on a board or plate and brush with the beaten egg. Season to taste with salt, pepper and garlic powder evenly over asparagus. Gently toss to coat evenly.
4. On a plate combine the bread crumbs and parmesan cheese. Toss seasoned asparagus in the bread crumb/parmesan mix, gently shaking off any excess coating.
5. Spray all sides of the breaded asparagus with oil spray. Dry breading might fly around in the air fryer and burn, so make sure to coat any dry spots.
6. Spray an air fryer basket/tray and place asparagus in the air fryer in a single layer.
7. Air Fry at 380°F/193°C for 5-8 minutes. Gently flip and spray any remaining dry spots with oil spray.
8. Air Fry at 380°F/193°C for additional 3-5 minutes or until crispy golden brown. Serve warm with your favorite dip.

# Baked Feta, Tomato & Garlic Pasta

Servings: 2

**Ingredients:**

- 100 g/3½ oz. feta or plant-based feta, cubed
- 20 cherry tomatoes
- 2 garlic cloves, peeled and halved
- ¾ teaspoon oregano
- 1 teaspoon chilli/hot red pepper flakes
- ½ teaspoon garlic salt
- 2 tablespoons olive oil
- 100 g/3½ oz. cooked pasta plus about 1 tablespoon of cooking water
- freshly ground black pepper

**Directions:**

1. Preheat the air-fryer to 200ºC/400ºF.
2. Place the feta, tomatoes and garlic in a baking dish that fits inside your air-fryer. Top with the oregano, chilli/hot red pepper flakes, garlic salt and olive oil. Place the dish in the preheated air-fryer and air-fry for 10 minutes, then remove and stir in the pasta and cooking water. Serve sprinkled with black pepper.

# Air Fryer Parsnips

Servings: 4
Cooking Time: 10 Mints
**Ingredients:**
- 450 g parsnips
- 2 tablespoons light olive oil
- ½ teaspoon salt
- 1 tablespoon liquid honey

**Directions:**
1. Preheat air fryer to 200°C/400°F.
2. Cut parsnips into 2-3 inch pieces, and place in a large bowl with the oil and salt. Toss to coat.
3. Place parsnips in an air fryer basket.
4. Optional: drizzle honey over the parsnips.
5. Air fry parsnips 10-15 minutes until tender and golden brown.

# Vegan Meatballs

Servings:4
Cooking Time:15 Minutes
**Ingredients:**
- 2 tbsp olive oil
- 2 tbsp soy sauce
- 1 onion, finely sliced
- 1 large carrot, peeled and grated
- 1 x 400 g / 14 oz can chickpeas, drained and rinsed
- 50 g / 1.8 oz plain flour
- 50 g / 1.8 oz rolled oats
- 2 tbsp roasted cashews, chopped
- 1 tsp garlic powder
- ½ tsp cumin

**Directions:**
1. Preheat the air fryer to 175 °C / 350 °F and line the air fryer with parchment paper or grease it with olive oil.
2. In a large mixing bowl, combine the olive oil and soy sauce. Add the onion slices and grated carrot and toss to coat in the sauce.
3. Place the vegetables in the air fryer and cook for 5 minutes until slightly soft.
4. Meanwhile, place the chickpeas, plain flour, rolled oats, and roasted cashews in a blender, and mix until well combined.
5. Remove the mixture from the blender and stir in the garlic powder and cumin. Add the onions and carrots to the bowl and mix well.
6. Scoop the mixture into small meatballs and place them into the air fryer. Increase the temperature on the machine up to 190 °C / 370 °F and cook the meatballs for 10-12 minutes until golden and crispy.

# Veggie Lasagne

Servings: 1

**Ingredients:**
- 2 lasagne sheets
- Pinch of salt
- 100g pasta sauce
- 50g ricotta
- 60g chopped basil
- 40g chopped spinach
- 3 tbsp grated courgette

**Directions:**
1. Break the lasagne sheets in half, bring a pan of water to boil
2. Cook the lasagne sheets for about 8 minutes, drain and pat dry
3. Add 2 tbsp of pasta sauce to a mini loaf tin
4. Add a lasagne sheet, top with ricotta, basil and spinach, then add courgette
5. Place another lasagne sheet on top
6. Add a couple of tbsp pasta sauce, basil, spinach and courgette
7. Add the last lasagne sheet, top with pasta sauce and ricotta
8. Cover with foil and place in the air fryer
9. Cook at 180°C for 10 mins, remove foil and cook for another 3 minutes

# Roast Cauliflower & Broccoli

Servings: 6

**Ingredients:**
- 300g broccoli
- 300g cauliflower
- 2 tbsp oil
- ½ tsp garlic powder
- ¼ tsp salt
- ¼ tsp paprika
- ⅛ tsp pepper

**Directions:**
1. Preheat air fryer to 200°C
2. Place broccoli and cauliflower in a bowl and microwave for 3 minutes
3. Add remaining ingredients and mix well
4. Add to the air fryer and cook for about 12 mins

# Crispy Potato Peels

Servings: 1

**Ingredients:**
- Peels from 4 potatoes
- Cooking spray
- Salt to season

**Directions:**
1. Heat the air fryer to 200°C
2. Place the peels in the air fryer spray with oil and sprinkle with salt
3. Cook for about 6-8 minutes until crispy

# Air Fryer Green Beans

Servings: 2
Cooking Time: 10 Mints

**Ingredients:**
- 80 g of green beans per person
- Spray oil
- Salt and pepper

**Directions:**
1. Add to a bowl.
2. Use a few sprays of spray oil.
3. Add salt and pepper.
4. Toss gently to ensure even coverage.
5. Pre-heat your air fryer to 200°C/400°F.
6. Add the green beans to the air fryer basket.
7. Cook for 6 minutes. Stir at least once during cooking.

# Roasted Vegetable Pasta

Servings:4
Cooking Time:15 Minutes

**Ingredients:**
- 400 g / 14 oz penne pasta
- 1 courgette, sliced
- 1 red pepper, deseeded and sliced
- 100 g / 3.5 oz mushroom, sliced
- 2 tbsp olive oil
- 1 tsp Italian seasoning
- 200 g cherry tomatoes, halved
- 2 tbsp fresh basil, chopped
- ½ tsp black pepper

**Directions:**
1. Cook the pasta according to the packet instructions.
2. Preheat the air fryer to 190 °C / 370 °F and line the air fryer with parchment paper or grease it with olive oil.
3. In a bowl, place the courgette, pepper, and mushroom, and toss in 2 tbsp olive oil
4. Place the vegetables in the air fryer and cook for 15 minutes.
5. Once the vegetables have softened, mix with the penne pasta, chopped cherry tomatoes, and fresh basil.
6. Serve while hot with a sprinkle of black pepper in each dish.

# Crispy Broccoli

Servings: 2
Cooking Time: X

**Ingredients:**
- 170 g/6 oz. broccoli florets
- 2 tablespoons olive oil
- ⅛ teaspoon garlic salt
- ⅛ teaspoon freshly ground black pepper
- 2 tablespoons freshly grated Parmesan or Pecorino

**Directions:**
1. Preheat the air-fryer to 200ºC/400ºF.
2. Toss the broccoli in the oil, season with the garlic salt and pepper, then toss over the grated cheese and combine well. Add the broccoli to the preheated air-fryer and air-fry for 5 minutes, giving the broccoli a stir halfway through to ensure even cooking.

# Spring Ratatouille

Servings:2
Cooking Time:15 Minutes

**Ingredients:**
- 1 tbsp olive oil
- 4 Roma tomatoes, sliced
- 2 cloves garlic, minced
- 1 courgette, cut into chunks
- 1 red pepper and 1 yellow pepper, cut into chunks
- 2 tbsp mixed herbs
- 1 tbsp vinegar

**Directions:**
1. Preheat the air fryer to 190 °C / 370 °F and line the air fryer with parchment paper or grease it with olive oil.
2. Place all of the ingredients into a large mixing bowl and mix until fully combined.
3. Transfer the vegetables into the lined air fryer basket, close the lid, and cook for 15 minutes until the vegetables have softened.

# Roast Vegetables

Servings: 4

**Ingredients:**
- 100g diced courgette
- 100g diced squash
- 100g diced mushrooms
- 100g diced cauliflower
- 100g diced asparagus
- 100g diced pepper
- 2 tsp oil
- ½ tsp salt
- ¼ tsp pepper
- ¼ tsp seasoning

**Directions:**
1. Preheat air fryer to 180°C
2. Mix all ingredients together
3. Add to air fryer and cook for 10 minutes stirring halfway

# Air Fryer Muchrooms

Servings: 2
Cooking Time: 35 Mints
**Ingredients:**
- 4 large flat mushrooms
- 2 tsp chopped fresh tarragon
- 50 g garlic butter, chopped
- Select all ingredients

**Directions:**
1. Heat air fryer to 180°C/350°F. Place the mushrooms, base-side up, in the air fryer basket. Sprinkle with fresh tarragon. Spray with oil and place the garlic butter on the gills of the mushrooms. Cook for 5 minutes.

# Baked Aubergine Slices With Yogurt Dressing

Servings: 2
**Ingredients:**
- 1 aubergine/eggplant, sliced 1.5 cm/⅝ in. thick
- 3 tablespoons olive oil
- ½ teaspoon salt
- YOGURT DRESSING
- 1 small garlic clove
- 1 tablespoon tahini or nut butter
- 100 g/½ cup Greek yogurt
- 2 teaspoons freshly squeezed lemon juice
- 1 tablespoon runny honey
- a pinch of salt
- a pinch of ground cumin
- a pinch of sumac
- TO SERVE
- 30 g/1 oz. rocket/arugula
- 2 tablespoons freshly chopped mint
- 3 tablespoons pomegranate seeds

**Directions:**
1. Preheat the air-fryer to 180ºC/350ºF.
2. Drizzle the olive oil over each side of the aubergine/eggplant slices. Sprinkle with salt. Add the aubergines to the preheated air-fryer and air-fry for 10 minutes, turning halfway through cooking.
3. Meanwhile, make the dressing by combining all the ingredients in a mini food processor (alternatively, finely chop the garlic, add to a jar with the other ingredients and shake vigorously).
4. Serve the cooked aubergine slices on a bed of rocket/arugula, drizzled with the dressing and with the mint and pomegranate seeds scattered over the top.

# Patatas Bravas

Servings: 4
Cooking Time: X

**Ingredients:**

- 750 g/1 lb. 10 oz. baby new potatoes
- 1 tablespoon olive oil
- ¼ teaspoon salt
- freshly chopped flat-leaf parsley, to garnish
- SAUCE
- 1 tablespoon olive oil
- 1 small red onion, finely diced
- 2–3 garlic cloves, crushed
- 1 tablespoon smoked paprika
- ¼ teaspoon cayenne pepper
- 400-g/14-oz. can chopped tomatoes
- 4 pitted green olives, halved
- ½ teaspoon salt

**Directions:**

1. Preheat the air-fryer to 200°C/400°F.
2. Rinse the potatoes and chop them to the same size as the smallest potato, then toss in the olive oil and sprinkle with the salt. Place the potatoes in the preheated air-fryer and air-fry for 18 minutes. Toss or shake the potatoes in the drawer halfway through.
3. While the potatoes are cooking, make the sauce. Heat the olive oil in a saucepan over a medium heat. Add the onion and sauté for about 5 minutes. Add the garlic, paprika and cayenne and cook for 1 minute. Add the tomatoes, olives and salt, plus 125 ml/½ cup water and simmer for about 20 minutes, until thickened. Purée the sauce in a blender or food processor.
4. Serve the potatoes in a bowl with the sauce poured over and the chopped parsley scattered over the top.

# Chapter 8 Side Dishes Recipes

## Spicy Green Beans

Servings: 4

**Ingredients:**

- 300g green beans
- 1 tbsp sesame oil
- 1 tsp soy
- 1 tsp rice wine vinegar
- 1 clove garlic, minced
- 1 tsp red pepper flakes

**Directions:**

1. Preheat air fryer to 200°C
2. Place green beans in a bowl
3. Mix together remaining ingredients, add green beans and fully coat
4. Place in the air fryer and cook for 12 minutes

# Air Fryer Eggy Bread

Servings:2
Cooking Time:5-7 Minutes

**Ingredients:**
- 4 slices white bread
- 4 eggs, beaten
- 1 tsp black pepper
- 1 tsp dried chives

**Directions:**
1. Preheat your air fryer to 150 °C / 300 °F and line the bottom of the basket with parchment paper.
2. Whisk the eggs in a large mixing bowl and soak each slice of bread until fully coated.
3. Transfer the eggy bread to the preheated air fryer and cook for 5-7 minutes until the eggs are set and the bread is crispy.
4. Serve hot with a sprinkle of black pepper and chives on top.

# Cheesy Garlic Asparagus

Servings: 4

**Ingredients:**
- 1 tsp olive oil
- 500g asparagus
- 1 tsp garlic salt
- 1 tbsp grated parmesan cheese
- Salt and pepper for seasoning

**Directions:**
1. Preheat the air fryer to 270°C
2. Clean the asparagus and cut off the bottom 1"
3. Pat dry and place in the air fryer, covering with the oil
4. Sprinkle the parmesan and garlic salt on top, seasoning to your liking
5. Cook for between 7 and 10 minutes
6. Add a little extra parmesan over the top before serving

# Courgette Chips

Servings: 4

**Ingredients:**
- 250g panko bread crumbs
- 100g grated parmesan
- 1 medium courgette, thinly sliced
- 1 egg beaten

**Directions:**
1. Preheat the air fryer to 175°C
2. Combine the breadcrumbs and parmesan
3. Dip the courgette into the egg then coat in bread crumbs
4. Spray with cooking spray and cook in the air fryer for 10 minutes
5. Turnover with tongs and cook for a further 2 minutes

# Homemade Croquettes

Servings: 4
Cooking Time: 15 Minutes

**Ingredients:**
- 400 g / 14 oz white rice, uncooked
- 1 onion, sliced
- 2 cloves garlic, finely sliced
- 2 eggs, beaten
- 50 g / 3.5 oz parmesan cheese, grated
- 1 tsp salt
- 1 tsp black pepper
- 50 g / 3.5 oz breadcrumbs
- 1 tsp dried oregano

**Directions:**
1. In a large mixing bowl, combine the white rice, onion slices, garlic cloves slices, one beaten egg, parmesan cheese, and a sprinkle of salt and pepper.
2. Whisk the second egg in a separate bowl and place the breadcrumbs into another bowl.
3. Shape the mixture into 12 even croquettes and roll evenly in the egg, followed by the breadcrumbs.
4. Preheat the air fryer to 190 °C / 375 °F and line the bottom of the basket with parchment paper.
5. Place the croquettes in the lined air fryer basket and cook for 15 minutes, turning halfway through, until crispy and golden. Enjoy while hot as a side to your main dish.

# Grilled Bacon And Cheese

Servings: 2

**Ingredients:**
- 4 slices of regular bread
- 1 tbsp butter
- 2 slices cheddar cheese
- 5 slices bacon, pre-cooked
- 2 slices mozzarella cheese

**Directions:**
1. Place the butter into the microwave to melt
2. Spread the butter onto one side of the bread slices
3. Place one slice of bread into the fryer basket, with the buttered side facing downwards
4. Place the cheddar on top, followed by the bacon, mozzarella and the other slice of bread, with the buttered side facing upwards
5. Set your fryer to 170°C and cook the sandwich for 4 minutes
6. Turn the sandwich over and cook for another 3 minutes
7. Turn the sandwich out and serve whilst hot
8. Repeat with the other remaining sandwich

# Sweet Potato Tots

Servings: 24

**Ingredients:**
- 2 sweet potatoes, peeled
- ½ tsp cajun seasoning
- Olive oil cooking spray
- Sea salt to taste

**Directions:**
1. Boil the sweet potatoes in a pan for about 15 minutes, allow to cool
2. Grate the sweet potato and mix in the cajun seasoning
3. Form into tot shaped cylinders
4. Spray the air fryer with oil, place the tots in the air fryer
5. Sprinkle with salt and cook for 8 minutes at 200°C, turn and cook for another 8 minutes

# Potato Hay

Servings: 4

**Ingredients:**
- 2 potatoes
- 1 tbsp oil
- Salt and pepper to taste

**Directions:**
1. Cut the potatoes into spirals
2. Soak in a bowl of water for 20 minutes, drain and pat dry
3. Add oil, salt and pepper and mix well to coat
4. Preheat air fryer to 180°C
5. Add potatoes to air fryer and cook for 5 minutes, toss then cook for another 12 until golden brown

# Crispy Cinnamon French Toast

Servings: 2

Cooking Time: 5 Minutes

**Ingredients:**
- 4 slices white bread
- 4 eggs
- 200 ml milk (cow's milk, cashew milk, soy milk, or oat milk)
- 2 tbsp granulated sugar
- 1 tsp brown sugar
- 1 tsp vanilla extract
- ½ tsp ground cinnamon

**Directions:**
1. Preheat your air fryer to 150 °C / 300 °F and line the bottom of the basket with parchment paper.
2. Cut each of the bread slices into 2 even rectangles and set them aside.
3. In a mixing bowl, whisk together the 4 eggs, milk, granulated sugar, brown sugar, vanilla extract, and ground cinnamon.
4. Soak the bread pieces in the egg mixture until they are fully covered and soaked in the mixture.
5. Place the coated bread slices in the lined air fryer, close the lid, and cook for 4-5 minutes until the bread is crispy and golden.
6. Serve the French toast slices with whatever toppings you desire.

# Carrot & Parmesan Chips

Servings: 2

**Ingredients:**
- 180g carrots
- 1 tbsp olive oil
- 2 tbsp grated parmesan
- 1 crushed garlic clove
- Salt and pepper for seasoning

**Directions:**
1. Take a mixing bowl and add the olive oil and garlic, combining well
2. Remove the tops of the carrots and cut into halves, and then another half
3. Add the carrots to the bowl and toss well
4. Add the parmesan and coat the carrots well
5. Add the carrots to the air fryer and cook for 20 minutes at 220°C, shaking halfway through

# Pumpkin Fries

Servings: 4

**Ingredients:**
- 1 small pumpkin, seeds removed and peeled, cut into half inch slices
- 2 tsp olive oil
- 1 tsp garlic powder
- 1/2 tsp paprika
- A pinch of salt

**Directions:**
1. Take a large bowl and add the slices of pumpkin
2. Add the oil and all the seasonings. Toss to coat well
3. Place in the air fryer
4. Cook at 280°C for 15 minutes, until the chips are tender, shaking at the halfway point

# Bbq Beetroot Crisps

Servings:4
Cooking Time:5 Minutes

**Ingredients:**
- 400 g / 14 oz beetroot, sliced
- 2 tbsp olive oil
- 1 tbsp BBQ seasoning
- ½ tsp black pepper

**Directions:**
1. Preheat the air fryer to 180 °C / 350 °F and line the bottom of the basket with parchment paper.
2. Place the beetroot slices in a large bowl. Add the olive oil, BBQ seasoning, and black pepper, and toss to coat the beetroot slices on both sides.
3. Place the beetroot slices in the air fryer and cook for 5 minutes until hot and crispy.

# Shishito Peppers

Servings: 2

**Ingredients:**
- 200g shishito peppers
- Salt and pepper to taste
- ½ tbsp avocado oil
- 75g grated cheese
- 2 limes

**Directions:**
1. Rinse the peppers
2. Place in a bowl and mix with oil, salt and pepper
3. Place in the air fryer and cook at 175°C for 10 minutes
4. Place on a serving plate and sprinkle with cheese

# Cauliflower With Hot Sauce And Blue Cheese Sauce

Servings:2
Cooking Time:15 Minutes

**Ingredients:**

- For the cauliflower:
- 1 cauliflower, broken into florets
- 4 tbsp hot sauce
- 2 tbsp olive oil
- 1 tsp garlic powder
- ½ tsp salt
- ½ tsp black pepper
- 1 tbsp plain flour
- 1 tbsp corn starch
- For the blue cheese sauce:
- 50 g / 1.8 oz blue cheese, crumbled
- 2 tbsp sour cream
- 2 tbsp mayonnaise
- ½ tsp salt
- ½ tsp black pepper

**Directions:**
1. Preheat the air fryer to 180 °C / 350 °F and line the bottom of the basket with parchment paper.
2. In a bowl, combine the hot sauce, olive oil, garlic powder, salt, and black pepper until it forms a consistent mixture. Add the cauliflower to the bowl and coat in the sauce.
3. Stir in the plain flour and corn starch until well combined.
4. Transfer the cauliflower to the lined basket in the air fryer, close the lid, and cook for 12-15 minutes until the cauliflower has softened and is golden in colour.
5. Meanwhile, make the blue cheese sauce by combining all of the ingredients. When the cauliflower is ready, remove it from the air fryer and serve with the blue cheese sauce on the side.

# Garlic And Parsley Potatoes

Servings: 4

**Ingredients:**

- 500g baby potatoes, cut into quarters
- 1 tbsp oil
- 1 tsp salt
- ½ tsp garlic powder
- ½ tsp dried parsley

**Directions:**
1. Preheat air fryer to 175ºC
2. Combine potatoes and oil in a bowl
3. Add remaining ingredients and mix
4. Add to the air fryer and cook for about 25 minutes until golden brown, turning halfway through

# Cheesy Broccoli

Servings: 4
Cooking Time: 5 Minutes

**Ingredients:**
- 1 large broccoli head, broken into florets
- 4 tbsp soft cheese
- 1 tsp black pepper
- 50 g / 3.5 oz cheddar cheese, grated

**Directions:**
1. Preheat the air fryer to 150 °C / 300 °F and line the mesh basket with parchment paper or grease it with olive oil.
2. Wash and drain the broccoli florets and place in a bowl and stir in the soft cheese and black pepper to fully coat all of the florets.
3. Transfer the broccoli to the air fryer basket and sprinkle the cheddar cheese on top. Close the lid and cook for 5-7 minutes until the broccoli has softened and the cheese has melted.
4. Serve as a side dish to your favourite meal.

# Sweet And Sticky Parsnips And Carrots

Servings: 2
Cooking Time: 15 Minutes

**Ingredients:**
- 4 large carrots, peeled and chopped into long chunks
- 4 large parsnips, peeled and chopped into long chunks
- 1 tbsp olive oil
- 2 tbsp honey
- 1 tsp dried mixed herbs

**Directions:**
1. Preheat the air fryer to 150 °C / 300 °F and line the bottom of the basket with parchment paper.
2. Place the chopped carrots and parsnips in a large bowl and drizzle over the olive oil and honey. Sprinkle in some black pepper to taste and toss well to fully coat the vegetables.
3. Transfer the coated vegetables into the air fryer basket and shut the lid. Cook for 20 minutes until the carrots and parsnips and cooked and crispy.
4. Serve as a side with your dinner.

# Zingy Brussels Sprouts

Servings: 2

**Ingredients:**
- 1 tbsp avocado oil
- ½ tsp salt
- ½ tsp pepper
- 400g Brussels sprouts halved
- 1 tsp balsamic vinegar
- 2 tsp crumbled bacon

**Directions:**
1. Preheat air fryer to 175°C
2. Combine oil, salt and pepper in a bowl and mix well. Add Brussels sprouts
3. Place in the air fryer and cook for 5 minutes shake then cook for another 5 minutes
4. Sprinkle with balsamic vinegar and sprinkle with bacon

# Ranch-style Potatoes

Servings: 2

**Ingredients:**
- 300g baby potatoes, washed
- 1 tbsp olive oil
- 3 tbsp dry ranch seasoning

**Directions:**
1. Preheat the air fryer to 220°C
2. Cut the potatoes in half
3. Take a mixing bowl and combine the olive oil with the ranch seasoning
4. Add the potatoes to the bowl and toss to coat
5. Cook for 15 minutes, shaking halfway through

# Stuffing Filled Pumpkin

Servings: 2

**Ingredients:**
- 1/2 small pumpkin
- 1 diced parsnip
- 1 sweet potato, diced
- 1 diced onion
- 2 tsp dried mixed herbs
- 50g peas
- 1 carrot, diced
- 1 egg
- 2 minced garlic cloves

**Directions:**
1. Remove the seeds from the pumpkin
2. Combine all the other ingredients in a bowl
3. Stuff the pumpkin
4. Preheat the air fryer to 175°C
5. Place the pumpkin in the air fryer and cook for about 30 minutes

# Chapter 9 Desserts Recipes

## Special Oreos

Servings: 9

**Ingredients:**
- 100g pancake mix
- 25ml water
- Cooking spray
- 9 Oreos
- 1 tbsp icing sugar

**Directions:**
1. Mix pancake mix and water until well combined
2. Line the air fryer with parchment paper and spray with cooking spray
3. Preheat the air fryer to 200°C
4. Dip each cookie in the pancake mix and place in the air fryer
5. Cook for 5 minutes, turn and cook for a further 3 minutes
6. Sprinkle with icing sugar to serve

# Apple Crumble

Servings: 4

**Ingredients:**
- 2 apples (each roughly 175 g/6 oz.), cored and chopped into 2-cm/¾-in cubes
- 3 tablespoons unrefined sugar
- 100 g/1 cup jumbo rolled oats/old-fashioned oats
- 40 g/heaped ¼ cup flour (gluten-free if you wish)
- 1 heaped teaspoon ground cinnamon
- 70 g/scant ⅓ cup cold butter, chopped into small cubes

**Directions:**
1. Preheat the air-fryer to 180°C/350°F.
2. Scatter the apple pieces in a baking dish that fits your air-fryer, then sprinkle over 1 tablespoon sugar. Add the baking dish to the preheated air-fryer and air-fry for 5 minutes.
3. Meanwhile, in a bowl mix together the oats, flour, remaining sugar and cold butter. Use your fingertips to bring the crumble topping together.
4. Remove the baking dish from the air-fryer and spoon the crumble topping over the partially cooked apple. Return the baking dish to the air dryer and air-fry for a further 10 minutes. Serve warm or cold.

# Zebra Cake

Servings: 6

**Ingredients:**
- 115g butter
- 2 eggs
- 100g caster sugar
- 1 tbsp cocoa powder
- 100g self raising flour
- 30ml milk
- 1tsp vanilla

**Directions:**
1. Preheat air fryer to 160°C
2. Line a 6 inch baking tin
3. Beat together the butter and sugar until light and fluffy
4. Add eggs one at a time then add the vanilla and milk
5. Add the flour and mix well
6. Divide the mix in half
7. Add cocoa powder to half the mix and mix well
8. Add a scoop of each of the batters at a time until it's all in the tin, place in the air fryer and cook for 30 minutes

# Milk And White Chocolate Chip Air Fryer Donuts With Frosting

Servings: 4
Cooking Time: 10 Minutes

**Ingredients:**
- For the donuts:
- 200 ml milk (any kind)
- 50 g / 3.5 oz brown sugar
- 50 g / 3.5 oz granulated sugar
- 1 tbsp active dry yeast
- 2 tbsp olive oil
- 4 tbsp butter, melted
- 1 egg, beaten
- 1 tsp vanilla extract
- 400 g / 14 oz plain flour
- 4 tbsp cocoa powder
- 100 g / 3.5 oz milk chocolate chips
- For the frosting:
- 5 tbsp powdered sugar
- 2 tbsp cocoa powder
- 100 ml heavy cream
- 50 g / 1.8 oz white chocolate chips, melted

**Directions:**
1. To make the donuts, whisk together the milk, brown and granulated sugars, and active dry yeast in a bowl. Set aside for a few minutes while the yeast starts to get foamy.
2. Stir the melted butter, beaten egg, and vanilla extract into the bowl. Mix well until all of the ingredients are combined.
3. Fold in the plain flour and cocoa powder until a smooth mixture forms.
4. Lightly flour a clean kitchen top surface and roll the dough out. Gently knead the dough for 2-3 minutes until it becomes soft and slightly tacky.
5. Transfer the dough into a large mixing bowl and cover it with a clean tea towel or some tinfoil. Leave the dough to rise for around one hour in a warm place.
6. Remove the tea towel or tinfoil from the bowl and roll it out on a floured surface once again. Use a rolling pin to roll the dough into a one-inch thick circle.
7. Use a round cookie cutter to create circular donuts and place each one into a lined air fryer basket.
8. Once all of the donuts have been placed into the air fryer, turn the machine onto 150 °C / 300 °F and close the lid.
9. Cook the donuts for 8-10 minutes until they are slightly golden and crispy on the outside.
10. While the donuts are cooking in the air fryer, make the frosting by combining the powdered sugar, cocoa powder, heavy cream, and melted white chocolate chips in a bowl. Mix well until a smooth, sticky mixture forms.
11. When the donuts are cooked, remove them from the air fryer and set aside to cool for 5-10 minutes. Once cooled, evenly spread some frosting on the top layer of each one. Place in the fridge to set for at least one hour.
12. Enjoy the donuts hot or cold.

# Fruit Scones

Servings: 4

**Ingredients:**
- 225g self raising flour
- 50g butter
- 50g sultanas
- 25g caster sugar
- 1 egg
- A little milk

**Directions:**
1. Place the flour in a bowl and rub in the butter, add the sultanas and mix
2. Stir in the caster sugar
3. Add the egg and mix well
4. Add a little bit of milk at a time to form a dough
5. Shape the dough into scones
6. Place in the air fryer and bake at 180°C for 8 minutes

# Strawberry Lemonade Pop Tarts

Servings: 12

**Ingredients:**
- 300g whole wheat flour
- 225g white flour
- ¼ tsp salt
- 2 tbsp light brown sugar
- 300g icing sugar
- 2 tbsp lemon juice
- Zest of 1 lemon
- 150g cold coconut oil
- 1 tsp vanilla extract
- 75ml ice cold water
- Strawberry Jam
- 1 tsp melted coconut oil
- ¼ tsp vanilla extract
- Sprinkles

**Directions:**
1. In a bowl mix the flours, salt and sugar. Mix in the cold coconut oil
2. Add 1 tsp vanilla and 1 tbsp at a time of the ice cold water, mix until a dough is formed
3. Take the dough and roll out thinly on a floured surface. Cut into 5cm by 7cm rectangles
4. Place a tsp of jam in the centre of half the rectangles, wet the edges place another rectangle on the top and seal
5. Place in the air fryer and cook at 200°C for 10 minutes. Allow to cool
6. Mix the icing sugar, coconut oil, lemon juice and lemon zest in a bowl. Mix well. Top the pop tarts and add sprinkles to serve

# Chocolate Soufflé

Servings: 2

**Ingredients:**
- 150g semi sweet chocolate, chopped
- ¼ cup butter
- 2 eggs, separated
- 3 tbsp sugar
- ½ tsp vanilla extract
- 2 tbsp flour
- Icing sugar
- Whipped cream to serve

**Directions:**
1. Butter and sugar 2 small ramekins
2. Melt the chocolate and butter together
3. In another bowl beat the egg yolks, add the sugar and vanilla beat well
4. Drizzle in the chocolate mix well, add the flour and mix well
5. Preheat the air fryer to 165°C
6. Whisk the egg whites to soft peaks, gently fold into the chocolate mix a little at a time
7. Add the mix to ramekins and place in the air fryer. Cook for about 14 minutes
8. Dust with icing sugar, serve with whipped cream

# Lava Cakes

Servings: 4

**Ingredients:**
- 1 ½ tbsp self raising flour
- 3 ½ tbsp sugar
- 150g butter
- 150g dark chocolate, chopped
- 2 eggs

**Directions:**
1. Preheat the air fryer to 175°C
2. Grease 4 ramekin dishes
3. Melt chocolate and butter in the microwave for about 3 minutes
4. Whisk the eggs and sugar together until pale and frothy
5. Pour melted chocolate into the eggs and stir in the flour
6. Fill the ramekins ¾ full, place in the air fryer and cook for 10 minutes

# Thai Fried Bananas

Servings: 8

**Ingredients:**
- 4 ripe bananas
- 2 tbsp flour
- 2 tbsp rice flour
- 2 tbsp cornflour
- 2 tbsp desiccated coconut
- Pinch salt
- ½ tsp baking powder
- ½ tsp cardamon powder

**Directions:**
1. Place all the dry ingredients in a bowl and mix well. Add a little water at a time and combine to form a batter
2. Cut the bananas in half and then half again length wise
3. Line the air fryer with parchment paper and spray with cooking spray
4. Dip each banana piece in the batter mix and place in the air fryer
5. Cook at 200°C for 10 -15 minutes turning halfway
6. Serve with ice cream

# Key Lime Cupcakes

Servings: 6

**Ingredients:**
- 250g Greek yogurt
- 200g soft cheese
- 2 eggs
- Juice and rind of 2 limes
- 1 egg yolk
- ¼ cup caster sugar
- 1 tsp vanilla essence

**Directions:**
1. Mix the Greek yogurt and soft cheese together until smooth
2. Add the eggs and mix, add the lime juice, rind, vanilla and caster sugar and mix well
3. Fill 6 cupcake cases with the mix and place the rest to one side
4. Place in the air fryer and cook at 160°C for 10 minutes then another 10 minutes at 180°C
5. Place the remaining mix into a piping bag, once the cupcakes have cooled pipe on the top and place in the fridge to set

# Chocolate Dipped Biscuits

Servings: 6

**Ingredients:**
- 225g self raising flour
- 100g sugar
- 100g butter
- 50g milk chocolate
- 1 egg beaten
- 1 tsp vanilla essence

**Directions:**
1. Add the flour, butter and sugar to a bowl and rub together
2. Add the egg and vanilla, mix to form a dough
3. Split the dough into 6 and form into balls
4. Place in the air fryer cook at 180°C for 15 minutes
5. Melt the chocolate, dip the cooked biscuits into the chocolate and half cover

# Pecan & Molasses Flapjack

Servings: 9

**Ingredients:**
- 120 g/½ cup plus 2 teaspoons butter or plant-based spread, plus extra for greasing
- 40 g/2 tablespoons blackstrap molasses
- 60 g/5 tablespoons unrefined sugar
- 50 g/½ cup chopped pecans
- 200 g/1½ cups porridge oats/steelcut oats (not rolled or jumbo)

**Directions:**
1. Preheat the air-fryer to 180°C/350°F.
2. Grease and line a 15 x 15-cm/6 x 6-in. baking pan.
3. In a large saucepan melt the butter/spread, molasses and sugar. Once melted, stir in the pecans, then the oats. As soon as they are combined, tip the mixture into the prepared baking pan and cover with foil.
4. Place the foil-covered baking pan in the preheated air-fryer and air-fry for 10 minutes. Remove the foil, then cook for a further 2 minutes to brown the top. Leave to cool, then cut into 9 squares.

# Chocolate Souffle

Servings:2
Cooking Time:15 Minutes

**Ingredients:**
- 2 eggs
- 4 tbsp brown sugar
- 1 tsp vanilla extract
- 4 tbsp butter, melted
- 4 tbsp milk chocolate chips
- 4 tbsp flour

**Directions:**
1. Preheat the air fryer to 180 °C / 350 °F. Remove the mesh basket from the machine and line it with parchment paper.
2. Separate the egg whites from the egg yolks and place them in two separate bowls.
3. Beat the yolks together with the brown sugar, vanilla extract, melted butter, milk chocolate chips, and flour in a bowl. It should form a smooth, consistent mixture.
4. Whisk the egg whites until they form stiff peaks. In batches, fold the egg whites into the chocolate mixture.
5. Divide the batter evenly between two souffle dishes and place them in the lined air fryer basket.
6. Cook the souffle dishes for 15 minutes until hot and set.

# Banana Maple Flapjack

Servings:9

**Ingredients:**
- 100 g/7 tablespoons butter (or plant-based spread if you wish)
- 75 g/5 tablespoons maple syrup
- 2 ripe bananas, mashed well with the back of a fork
- 1 teaspoon vanilla extract
- 240 g/2½ cups rolled oats/quick-cooking oats

**Directions:**
1. Gently heat the butter and maple syrup in a medium saucepan over a low heat until melted. Stir in the mashed banana, vanilla and oats and combine all ingredients. Pour the flapjack mixture into a 15 x 15-cm/6 x 6-in. baking pan and cover with foil.
2. Preheat the air-fryer to 200°C/400°F.
3. Add the baking pan to the preheated air-fryer and air-fry for 12 minutes, then remove the foil and cook for a further 4 minutes to brown the top. Leave to cool before cutting into 9 squares.

# Tasty Cannoli

Servings: 4

**Ingredients:**

- 400g ricotta cheese
- 200g mascarpone cheese
- 150g icing sugar
- 160ml double cream
- 1 tsp vanilla extract
- 1 tsp orange zest
- 150g mini chocolate chips
- 350g flour
- 150g sugar
- 1 tsp salt
- 1/2 tsp cinnamon
- 6 tbsp white wine
- 1 egg, plus 1 extra egg white
- 4 tbsp cubed cold butter

**Directions:**

1. Take a large mixing bowl and a hand mixer. Combine the cream and half the icing sugar until you see stiff peaks starting to form
2. Take another bowl and combine the rest of the icing sugar with the ricotta, mascarpone, zest, salt and vanilla
3. Fold the ricotta mixture into the cream mixture carefully and place in the refrigerator for 1 hour
4. Take a large bowl and combine the cinnamon, salt, sugar and lour
5. Cut the butter into chunks and add to the mixture, combining well
6. Add the egg and the wine and combine until you see a dough starting to form
7. Cover the dough with plastic wrap and place in the refrigerator for 1 hour
8. Cut the dough into halves and roll each half into about 1/8" thickness
9. Use a cookie cutter (around 4" size) to cut out rounds
10. Wrap the cold dough around your cannoli moulds
11. Brush the seal with the egg white to hold it together
12. Preheat the air fryer to 220°C
13. Place the cannoli in the basket and cook for 12 minutes
14. Once cooled slightly, remove the moulds
15. Place the cream mixture into a pastry bag and pipe into the cannoli shells
16. Dip both ends into the chocolate chips for decoration

# Chocolate Cake

Servings: 2

**Ingredients:**

- 3 eggs
- 75ml sour cream
- 225g flour
- 150g sugar
- 2 tsp vanilla extract
- 25g cocoa powder
- 1 tsp baking powder
- ½ tsp baking soda

**Directions:**

1. Preheat the air fryer to 160°C
2. Mix all the ingredients together in a bowl
3. Pour into a greased baking tin
4. Place into the air fryer and cook for 25 minutes
5. Allow to cool and ice with chocolate frosting

# Lemon Tarts

Servings: 8

**Ingredients:**

- 100g butter
- 225g plain flour
- 30g caster sugar
- Zest and juice of 1 lemon
- 4 tsp lemon curd

**Directions:**

1. In a bowl mix together butter, flour and sugar until it forms crumbs, add the lemon zest and juice
2. Add a little water at a time and mix to form a dough
3. Roll out the dough and line 8 small ramekins with it
4. Add ¼ tsp of lemon curd to each ramekin
5. Cook in the air fryer for 15 minutes at 180°C

# Chocolate Orange Muffins

Servings: 12

**Ingredients:**
- 100g self raising flour
- 110g caster sugar
- 50g butter
- 20g cocoa powder
- 50ml milk
- 1 tsp cocoa nibs
- 1 large orange juice and rind
- 1 tbsp honey
- 1tsp vanilla essence
- 2 eggs

**Directions:**
1. Add the flour, butter and sugar to a mixing bowl and rug together
2. Add the cocoa, honey, orange and vanilla mix well
3. Mix the milk and egg together then add to the flour mix, combine well
4. Rub your muffin cases with flour to stop them sticking, add 2 tbsp batter to each one
5. Cook in the air fryer for 12 minutes at 180°C

# Melting Moments

Servings: 9

**Ingredients:**
- 100g butter
- 75g caster sugar
- 150g self raising flour
- 1 egg
- 50g white chocolate
- 3 tbsp desiccated coconut
- 1 tsp vanilla essence

**Directions:**
1. Preheat the air fryer to 180°C
2. Cream together the butter and sugar, beat in the egg and vanilla
3. Bash the white chocolate into small pieces
4. Add the flour and chocolate and mix well
5. Roll into 9 small balls and cover in coconut
6. Place in the air fryer and cook for 8 minutes and a further 6 minutes at 160°C

# Banana Bread

Servings: 8

**Ingredients:**
- 200g flour
- 1 tsp cinnamon
- ½ tsp salt
- ¼ tsp baking soda
- 2 ripe banana mashed
- 2 large eggs
- 75g sugar
- 25g plain yogurt
- 2 tbsp oil
- 1 tsp vanilla extract
- 2 tbsp chopped walnuts
- Cooking spray

**Directions:**
1. Line a 6 inch cake tin with parchment paper and coat with cooking spray
2. Whisk together flour, cinnamon, salt and baking soda set aside
3. In another bowl mix together remaining ingredients, add the flour mix and combine well
4. Pour batter into the cake tin and place in the air fryer
5. Cook at 155°C for 35 minutes turning halfway through

# Recipe Index

## A

Air Feyer Breaded Asparagus Fries 66

Air Fryer 2-inigrdient Sweet Potato Roll: No Yeast 25

Air Fryer Bacon Wrapped Zucchini Fries 27

Air Fryer Bacon-wrapped Asparagus 50

Air Fryer Chicken Breast 37

Air Fryer Chicken Parmesan 40

Air Fryer Chicken Tenders 42

Air Fryer Chicken Wings 35

Air Fryer Chicken Wings With Honey And Sesame 41

Air Fryer Chili Cheese Hotdogs 31

Air Fryer Crab Cakes 57

Air Fryer Eggy Bread 74

Air Fryer Fish Fillets 60

Air Fryer Frozen Breadsticks 30

Air Fryer Frozen Chicken Cordon Bleu 38

Air Fryer Green Beans 69

Air Fryer Hot Dogs 23

Air Fryer Lamb Steaks 45

Air Fryer Lemon Pepper Shrimp 59

Air Fryer Muchrooms 72

Air Fryer Orange Shrimp & Broccol 54

Air Fryer Parsnips 67

Air Fryer Party Snack Mix-"nuts & Bolts" 29

Air Fryer Rack Of Lamb 44

Air Fryer Rosemary Chicken Breast 32

Air Fryer Rotisserie Chicken 39

Air Fryer Spicy Bay Scallops 53

Air Fryer Tikka Chicken Breast 41

Air Fryer Trader Joe's Frozen Kung Pao Chicken 32

Air Fryer Tuna 61

Apple Crumble 84

Apricot Lamb Burgers 47

## B

Baba Ganoush 22

Bacon Smokies 24

Baked Aubergine Slices With Yogurt Dressing 72

Baked Feta, Tomato & Garlic Pasta 66

Banana Bread 94

Banana Maple Flapjack 90

Bbq Beetroot Crisps 79

Bbq Chicken Tenders 38

Beef Nacho Pinwheels 52

Beef Stirfry 45

Beetroot Crisps 26

Blanket Breakfast Eggs 18

Blueberry & Lemon Breakfast Muffins 21

Breakfast Sausage Burgers 19

Buffalo Wings 39

## C

Carrot & Parmesan Chips 78

Cauliflower With Hot Sauce And Blue Cheese Sauce 80

Cheddar & Bbq Stuffed Chicken 37

Cheesy Broccoli 81

Cheesy Garlic Asparagus 74

Cheesy Sausage Breakfast Pockets 14

Cheesy Taco Crescents 23

Chicken Milanese 34

Chinese Pork With Pineapple 43

Chocolate Cake 92

Chocolate Dipped Biscuits 89

Chocolate Orange Muffins 93

Chocolate Soufflé 87

Chocolate Souffle 90

Coconut Shrimp 56

Cod In Parma Ham 58

Copycat Fish Fingers 56
Courgette Chips 75
Crispy Broccoli 70
Crispy Cinnamon French Toast 77
Crispy Potato Peels 69
Crunchy Mexican Breakfast Wrap 20

# E

Easy Air Fryer Sausage 13
Easy Cheese & Bacon Toasties 15
Easy Cheesy Scrambled Eggs 15
Egg & Bacon Breakfast Cups 20
European Pancakes 16

# F

Fish In Foil 55
Fish Sticks With Tartar Sauce Batter 60
Focaccia Bread 27
French Toast 18
Fruit Scones 86

# G

Garlic And Parsley Potatoes 80
Garlic Butter Salmon 59
Gluten Free Honey And Garlic Shrimp 63
Grilled Bacon And Cheese 76

# H

Hawaiian Chicken 33
Healthy Stuffed Peppers 14
Homemade Croquettes 75
Honey & Mustard Meatballs 51

# I

Italian Meatballs 46

# K

Key Lime Cupcakes 88

# L

Lamb Koftas 52
Lava Cakes 87
Lemon Pepper Shrimp 53
Lemon Tarts 92
Lentil Burgers 63
Loaded Hash Browns 12

# M

Meaty Egg Cups 12
Melting Moments 93
Mexican Breakfast Burritos 16
Milk And White Chocolate Chip Air Fryer Donuts With Frosting 85
Mini Moroccan Lamb Burgers 48
Mongolian Beef 49
Monte Cristo Breakfast Sandwich 21

# O

Oat & Parmesan Crusted Fish Fillets 61
Olive Stained Turkey Breast 36
Oozing Baked Eggs 19
Orange Zingy Cauliflower 65

# P

Paneer Tikka 64
Pao De Queijo 25
Patatas Bravas 73
Pecan & Molasses Flapjack 89
Peppery Lemon Shrimp 58
Pesto Salmon 54
Plantain Fries 22
Pork Chops With Sprouts 47
Pork Jerky 26
Pork With Chinese 5 Spice 48
Potato & Chorizo Frittata 13
Potato Hay 77
Pretzel Bites 28
Pulled Pork, Bacon, And Cheese Sliders 51
Pumpkin Fries 78

## Q

Quick Chicken Nuggets 36

## R

Rainbow Vegetables 64

Ranch-style Potatoes 82

Raspberry Breakfast Pockets 17

Roast Cauliflower & Broccoli 68

Roast Vegetables 71

Roasted Vegetable Pasta 70

## S

Salmon Patties 62

Salt And Pepper Belly Pork 49

Satay Chicken Skewers 34

Shishito Peppers 79

Shrimp With Yum Yum Sauce 55

Simple Steaks 44

Snack Style Falafel 30

Special Oreos 83

Spicy Chicken Wing Drummettes 33

Spicy Green Beans 73

Spinach And Feta Croissants 65

Spring Ratatouille 71

Spring Rolls 28

Steak Popcorn Bites 43

Sticky Asian Beef 46

Sticky Chicken Tikka Drumsticks 35

Store-cupboard Fishcakes 62

Strawberry Lemonade Pop Tarts 86

Stuffed Mushrooms 29

Stuffing Filled Pumpkin 83

Sweet And Sticky Parsnips And Carrots 81

Sweet Potato Fries 24

Sweet Potato Tots 76

## T

Tangy Breakfast Hash 17

Tasty Cannoli 91

Thai Fried Bananas 88

Traditional Empanadas 50

## V

Vegan Meatballs 67

Veggie Lasagne 68

## W

Whole Mini Peppers 31

## Z

Zebra Cake 84

Zingy Brussels Sprouts 82

Printed in Great Britain
by Amazon